LIVING

D0890324

Also available in Vintage Living Texts

Martin Amis

Margaret Atwood

Louis de Bernières

Sebastian Faulks

John Fowles

Susan Hill

Ian McEwan

Toni Morrison

Salman Rushdie

Jeanette Winterson

VINTAGE LIVING TEXTS

American Fiction

THE ESSENTIAL GUIDE TO CONTEMPORARY LITERATURE

Native Son – Richard Wright

To Kill A Mockingbird – Harper Lee

The Catcher in the Rye – J. D. Salinger

Catch-22 – Joseph Heller

V
VINTAGE

Published by Vintage 2003

2 4 6 8 10 9 7 5 3 1

First published in Great Britain in 2003 by Vintage
Random House, 20 Vauxhall Bridge Road,
London SW1V 2SA

Random House Australia (Pty) Limited
20 Alfred Street, Milsons Point, Sydney,
New South Wales 2061, Australia

Random House New Zealand Limited
18 Poland Road, Glenfield,
Auckland 10, New Zealand

Random House (Pty) Limited
Endulini, 5A Jubilee Road, Parktown 2193, South Africa

The Random House Group Limited Reg. No. 954009
www.randomhouse.co.uk

A CIP catalogue record for this book is available from the British Library

ISBN 0 09 9445069

Papers used by Random House are natural, recyclable products made
from wood grown in sustainable forests. The manufacturing processes
conform to the environmental regulations of the country of origin.

Typeset by Palimpsest Book Production Limited, Polmont, Stirlingshire

Printed and bound in Great Britain by
Bookmarque Ltd, Croydon, Surrey

CONTENTS

VINTAGE LIVING TEXTS: PREFACE

About this series : 1
Content : 1
How to use this series : 2
Who are these books for? : 3

AMERICAN FICTION

Introduction : 5
Interviews and silences: selections from interviews : 13
with Richard Wright, Harper Lee, J. D. Salinger
and Joseph Heller

VINTAGE LIVING TEXTS

Native Son

Reading activities: detailed analysis : 43
Contexts, comparisons and complementary readings : 81

To Kill a Mockingbird

Reading activities: detailed analysis : 91
Contexts, comparisons and complementary readings : 131

The Catcher in the Rye

141 : Reading activities: detailed analysis
173 : Contexts, comparisons and complementary readings

Catch-22

181 : Reading activities: detailed analysis
209 : Contexts, comparisons and complementary readings

VINTAGE LIVING TEXTS: REFERENCE

217 : Glossary of literary terms used in this book
225 : Biographical outline: principal dates for Richard Wright, Harper Lee, J. D. Salinger and Joseph Heller
229 : Select bibliography

Acknowledgements

We owe grateful thanks to all at Random House. Most of all our debt is to Rachel Cugnoni and her team at Vintage – especially Ali Reynolds – Jason Arthur and Liz Foley, who have given us generous and unfailing support. Thanks also to Caroline Michel, Marcella Edwards, Philippa Brewster and Georgina Capel, Michael Meredith, Angela Leighton, Harriet Marland, to all our colleagues and friends, and to our partners and families. We would also like to thank the teachers and students at schools and colleges around the country who have taken part in our trialling process, and who have responded so readily and warmly to our requests for advice. And finally, our thanks to the four authors featured here.

VINTAGE
LIVING
TEXTS

Preface

About this series

Vintage Living Texts: The Essential Guide to Contemporary Literature is a new concept in reading guides. Our aim is to provide readers of all kinds with an intelligent and accessible introduction to key works of contemporary literature. Each guide suggests techniques for reading important contemporary novels, and offers a variety of back-up materials that will give you ways into the text – without ever telling you what to think.

Content

Usually the books reproduce an extensive interview with the author, conducted exclusively for this series. This is not to say that we believe that the author's word is law. Of course it isn't. Once his or her book has gone out into the world he or she becomes simply yet another – if singularly competent – reader. This series recognises that an author's contribution may be valuable, and intriguing, but it puts the reader in control.

In the case of *American Fiction* we have included an account drawn from published interviews with, or prefaces by, Harper Lee, Richard Wright and Joseph Heller to offer some perspective on their literary opinions, methods and preoccupations.

For J. D. Salinger we have included an account of his silence on his work and treated that silence as, in itself, a comment.

Most of the titles in the series are author-focused and cover at least three novels by that writer, along with relevant biographical, bibliographical, contextual and comparative material. With *American Fiction* we are catering for a particular school and college audience who often study these four key works of twentieth-century fiction, either together or separately.

How to use this series

In the reading plans that make up the core of each book you will see that you are asked to do two things. One comes from the text; that is, we suggest what you should focus on, whether it's a theme, the language or the narrative method. The other concentrates on your own response. We want you to think about how you are reading and what skills you are bringing to bear in doing that reading. So this part is very much about you, the reader.

The point is that there are many ways of responding to a text. You could concentrate on the methods you might use to compare this text with others. In which case, look for the sections headed 'Compare'. Or you might want to do something more individual, and analyse how you are reacting to a text and what it means to you, in which case, pick out the approaches labelled 'Imagine' or 'Make up' or 'Write'.

Of course, it may well be that you are reading these texts for an exam. In that case, you will have to go for the more traditional methods of literary criticism and look for the responses that tell you to 'Discuss' or 'Analyse'. But whichever level you (or your students) are at, you will find that there is something here for everyone. However, we're not suggesting that you stick solely to the approaches we offer, or that you tackle all of the exercises laid out here. Choose whatever most interests you, or whatever best suits your purposes.

Who are these books for?

Students will find that these guides will be like a good teacher. They introduce the life and work of the author, set each novel in its context, explain key ideas and literary critical terms as they arise, suggest comparative exercises in a number of media, and ask focused questions to encourage a well-informed, analytical approach to reading the novels in a way that is rigorous, but still entertaining.

Teachers will find in this series a rich source of ideas for teaching contemporary novels and their contexts, particularly at AS, A and undergraduate levels. The exercises on each text have been tailored to meet the various assessment objectives laid down in the subject criteria for GCE AS and for GCE A-level and International Baccalaureate English Literature, and are explained in such a way that they can be easily selected and fitted into a lesson plan. Given the diversity of ways that the awarding bodies have devised their specifications to meet these assessment objectives, a wide range of exercises is offered. We've had fun devising the plans, and hope that they'll be fun for you when you come to teach and learn with them.

And if you are neither a teacher nor a student of contemporary literature, but someone reading for your own pleasure? Well, if you've ever wanted someone to introduce you to a novelist's work in a way that will let you trust your own judgement and read more confidently, then this guide is also for you.

Whoever you are, we hope that you will enjoy using these books and that they will send you back to the novels to find new pleasures.

All page references to *Native Son, To Kill a Mockingbird* and *Catch-22* refer to the Vintage editions. Page references to *The Catcher in the Rye* refer to the paperback Penguin edition.

American Fiction

Introduction

'The truth about Salinger was always there, in his fiction.'

One of the guiding principles of the *Vintage Living Texts* series is to establish the idea of the author as a 'reader' of his or her own fictions. We suggest that the authors offer insights into their fiction, but that they provide no definitive version of their own texts. You, the reader, should be in charge of your own interpretation. As an intelligent reader you draw upon as many resources – historical, literary, biographical or personal – as you possibly can to make your reading as sophisticated as it can be.

This text has particular differences from the rest of the *Vintage Living Texts* series, as there is no exclusive interview with any of the writers included. However, this provides a special opportunity to focus on what it means to 'speak to', or read an interview with, an author. 'Interviews and silences' examines how you deal with the comments of an author, as it analyses Richard Wright's essay 'How "Bigger" Was Born' (which is included in your Vintage edition of the novel). It also considers the consequence of an author's silence or refusal to speak on their own text. The introduction, therefore, leaves the discussion of the author's role to 'Interviews and silences', and, instead, offers you a concise biography of the four authors featured here. It then takes you through the conceptual link that brings reading guides for *Native Son, To Kill a Mockingbird, The Catcher in the Rye* and *Catch-22* together in one text.

The first text covered in this collection is Richard Wright's *Native Son*. Originally published in March 1940, it became an instant best-seller. Born in 1908 in Natchez, Mississippi, Wright was the older of two boys and raised by his mother, his father having left when the boys were small. Wright's childhood was framed by the necessity of moving from town to town while his mother searched for work, and by the segregation laws of the Southern states. He fled the South and its treatment of the black population, and settled in Chicago at the age of nineteen. In Chicago he struggled to find work, read avidly, and became an active member of the Communist Party. The influence of this political affiliation is clear in *Native Son*.

Six years after the publication of *Native Son*, Wright published his memoir, entitled *Black Boy*, and in its successful aftermath he visited France, where he was to settle for the rest of his life. Wright became a central member of the Paris literati, associating with the likes of James Baldwin and Simone de Beauvoir.

In terms of Wright's literary heritage *Native Son* is, by far, his most famous novel, but *Uncle Tom's Children* – written in response to Harriet Beecher Stowe's *Uncle Tom's Cabin* – is also important. This text helps the reader to establish what Wright is writing against, what he disassociates himself from, as well as his political aspirations as revealed in *Native Son*. He spent the majority of his writing life attempting to present to the reader the frameworks of oppression he identified. Wright did not regard 'racism' as a Southern or even an American problem, but rather as a hierarchy securing white cultural and political supremacy.

Wright died at the age of fifty-two, in 1960, the year Harper Lee's novel, also about the segregated South in 1930s America, was published. Harper Lee was born on 28 April 1926 in Monroeville, Alabama. The youngest of a family of four, she was educated in both Alabama and England (she attended Oxford University in the late 1940s). Initially composed in 1957, *To Kill a Mockingbird* was submitted to J. B. Lippincott & Co., who suggested she rewrite sections of her material. This rewriting took Lee two and a half years, and when her only novel was finally published, Lee was awarded the Pulitzer Prize for fiction. Apart from writing the odd article for American *Vogue*, she has gone on to publish very little.

While Lee is famous for her authorial silence, her literary connections are well publicised. Truman Capote, author – perhaps most famously – of *Breakfast at Tiffany's* and *In Cold Blood*, lived as a child next door to Lee. He is commonly thought to be the basis for the character of Dill, although, of course, Lee herself does not comment upon this association.

The text is closely allied to both Lee's personal and public history. Her understanding of her father's legal career (Amasa Coleman Lee was a lawyer) seems to have influenced her characterisation of Atticus, and her regard for the legal profession. Similarly, her treatment of the trial of the Scottsboro boys, a controversial case alleging the rape of two white girls by a gang of black boys, seems to have formed the substance of Lee's plot for her. It also appears to have influenced her treatment of Tom Robinson, and her meditation on the nature of false accusation. Lee's upbringing in Monroe County and the state of Alabama situates the novel both culturally and geographically.

J. D. Salinger's most famous novel, *The Catcher in the Rye*, is also framed by the author's childhood context. Salinger was born in New York City on 1 January 1919, and the biographical details of his life are notoriously difficult to authenticate.

7

As a child he attended the Valley Forge Military Academy in Pennsylvania, which, unlike his protagonist Holden Caulfield, he is believed to have very much enjoyed. His academic career included sojourns at Columbia University, New York University and the rather less famous Ursinus College; he also fought in the Second World War with the Twelfth Infantry Regiment. *The Catcher in the Rye*, first published in 1951, brought him a great deal of media attention, which he is rumoured to have used to attract numbers of young women. However, he quickly shunned his public profile and has subsequently lived the life of a 'recluse' in Cornish New Hampshire. His familial relationships are understood to be severely ruptured: it is commonly cited, for instance, that he did not attend his father's funeral; and in an interview with the online magazine *Salon*, his daughter Peggy spoke about their volatile relationship:

> [Peggy] reports that in the early 70s, after living with Salinger for eight months, she was unceremoniously booted out of his life. Eighteen years old to Salinger's 53, she spent the next 20 years wondering what it was that she had done . . . After an argument, Salinger told his daughter, 'I'll always love you, but when I lose respect for a person, I'm done with them. Finished.'
> http://dir.salon.com/books/feature/2000/10/02/salinger/index.html

Famed for his lack of interest in people, including his fans, Salinger's complicated relation with one other writer is particularly notorious. Ian Hamilton attempted to publish a biography of Salinger, which the author challenged in the courts. Hamilton then went on to use much of his biography in an account of his attempts to produce the biography itself, entitled *In Search of J. D. Salinger*.

Joseph Heller was born in New York in 1923 and served as a bombardier in the Second World War. Out of his experiences in the army came the fourth novel covered in this volume – *Catch-22*, published in 1961. Heller taught for a while at Pennsylvania State University, but he developed the idea for his most famous novel while working in the advertising departments of eminent magazines such as *Time, Look* and *McCall's*.

Heller's awareness of the growing significance of an American consumer culture, where everything is up for grabs, combined with the story of Ian Hamilton's public challenge to Salinger's right to privacy, provide one of the thematic links that bind the novels examined in this text. In order to protect his rights as an individual and a private person, Salinger took Hamilton to court and *won*, preventing Hamilton from publishing the text he had written. Salinger was protected by the American system of justice set in place to secure the rights of the individual. While *Catch-22* shows the crazy workings of an army system which denied the rights of the individual, Heller's theme places emphasis on the same cherished American ideal.

The idea of the trial, or court scene, as a means of achieving justice is one that Salinger has relied upon. It worked to protect him as a 'victim' of the intrusive journalist. In both *Native Son* and *To Kill a Mockingbird*, this idea is interrogated. The texts challenge the idea of the victim, suggesting that the men on trial – Bigger in *Native Son* and Tom Robinson in *To Kill a Mockingbird* – are not only the 'criminals' on trial, but also the *victims* of the culture in which they live. The novels explore the extent to which the justice system protects certain individuals at the expense of other American citizens. The authors take up very different positions in this debate, but they both wholeheartedly enter this complex arena, and use courtroom drama to put the ideas of justice, innocence and guilt on trial.

What it means to be 'innocent' is also a central concept in *The Catcher in the Rye*. The context, rather than being a courtroom, is the idea that part of adolescence is rebellion, but just as with Bigger and Tom, Holden's relationship to his crimes is complicated. He frequently asserts that his own actions are beyond his control and that he is therefore not responsible, or 'guilty', as a result. Similarly, in Heller's *Catch-22* an impossible contradiction in army rules means that individuality is denied and responsibility abrogated.

The second linking theme for these four books is the idea of the 'text', or story, as a powerful tool in the creation of cultural and social imperatives. In all four texts the idea of the 'story' and the power of narrative is central. In Lee's *To Kill a Mockingbird* the power of storytelling is nowhere more clearly demonstrated than in Mayella's 'story' about Tom Robinson. Her account of their relationship – the story she tells in court – ultimately leads to his death. But the importance of stories is reiterated throughout the novel: by Scout, Jem and Dill's 'stories' about Boo Radley, or in Jem's reluctant storytelling when he visits Mrs Dubose. Equally, in Salinger's *The Catcher in the Rye*, Holden constantly blurs the boundary between storytelling and any notion of 'truth'. The idea of the story is highlighted in its relationship to psychology and the idea of storytelling as therapy. This is epitomised in Holden's 'story' about Allie's glove. The characters fail to appreciate the importance of this story to Holden, but the reader is left in no doubt about the meaningful narratives throughout this novel, even if Holden insists on disguising them with heavy irony.

In *Native Son* Bigger provides a contrast to Holden Caulfield. Whereas Holden is perhaps uncontrollably creative, constantly (and consciously) referring to the narrative qualities of his life by mentioning other stories, Bigger is only confronted by narrative possibilities as he faces the electric chair. This novel argues for the force of narrative, not as a possibility for the individual, but rather as a possible form of oppression. (Much as the 'narrative' or the 'story' of army rules results in a form of oppression in Heller's *Catch-22*.) Bigger thinks the story of a black man's life is mapped out for him – he knows the possible plot twists and its grand finale. This is suggested by his game with Gus (pp. 46–52) where they fantasise about 'white' jobs and lifestyles; the story of their lives includes these narrative possibilities. The novel, polemic in style, unlike *The Catcher in the Rye*, or *To Kill a Mockingbird*, drives home to the reader the consequences of telling a community one story, of offering them restricted possibilities for their autobiography, and places the responsibility for that narrative squarely with the storyteller, not the protagonist.

These very different versions of the power of narrative offer up one key reminder to the reader. They suggest, in their various styles and subject matters, the fundamental importance of interpretation. They all encourage you, the reader, to *read* these narratives against the grain. Through irony (*The Catcher in the Rye* and *Catch-22*), sympathy (*Mockingbird*), or polemic (*Native Son*), they demand that you do not simply sit back and agree. This active understanding of reading runs through all four novels. They all ask the reader to take a questioning, creative approach, while demanding that you recognise the political, cultural, and – perhaps most importantly – personal force of narrative.

Interviews and silences

The *Vintage Living Texts* reading guides include, where possible, an interview with the author featured. In the case of this guide to four books by American authors widely studied in schools and colleges, one of the things that links these diverse writers is the fact that we cannot speak directly to the authors themselves. Richard Wright died in 1960, Joseph Heller in 1999; Harper Lee has been unwilling to speak about her work, and J. D. Salinger is, and always has been, notoriously reclusive.

In the first part of this section, Richard Wright's introduction to *Native Son*, 'How "Bigger" was Born', is 'transformed' by us into direct responses to specific questions. Wright's introduction as a whole is a valuable critical tool; here, however, it is restructured to help you trace particular critical concerns. You are given the page references for the introduction, in the Vintage edition, to help you orient yourself, but the question-and-answer format is designed to help you think about the introduction as a critical resource. For Joseph Heller we have used the same approach, devising questions that we – and, we hope, you – would have liked to ask Heller, and finding the answers in his published introduction to the 1994 Vintage edition of *Catch-22*. (You may find that this is a useful method when you are considering your own reading of other writers' published 'introductions' to their own work.)

Both Harper Lee and J. D. Salinger are still alive, but equally, both are famous for their refusal to give interviews, to comment on their fiction, or in fact to appear in public at all. This introduction, therefore, focuses on their silence. In the section on Harper Lee, you are given the perspective of another author on Lee. This is framed with a short discussion on her reluctance to comment herself, but her willingness to allow another author to introduce her work with a story of his own. In the section devoted to Salinger, the author's silence is itself the focus for discussion.

RICHARD WRIGHT

This invented 'interview' is a reworking and transformation of Wright's essay 'How "Bigger" was Born'. It examines Wright's responses to the kinds of critical issues that are important to the *Vintage Living Texts* series: the relationship of the reader to the text, the idea of the author controlling interpretation, and the nature and techniques of the novel's construction.

QUESTION: To what extent might you, as an author, consider yourself responsible or 'accountable' for the interpretation of a text?

RW: I am not so pretentious as to imagine that it is possible for me to account completely for my own book, *Native Son*. But I am going to try to account for as much of it as I can, the sources of it, the material that went into it, and my own years' long changing attitude toward that material. [...]

The more closely the author thinks of why he wrote, the more he comes to regard his imagination as a kind of self-generating cement which glues facts together, and his emotions as a kind of dark and obscure designer of those facts. Always there is something that is just beyond the tip of the tongue that could explain it all. Usually, he ends up by discussing something far afield, an act which incites skepticism and suspicion in those anxious for a straight-out explanation.

Yet the author is eager to explain. But the moment he makes the attempt his words falter, for he is confronted and defied by the inexplicable array of his own emotions. Emotions are subjective and he can communicate them only when he clothes them in an objective guise; and how can he ever be so arrogant as to know when he is dressing up the right emotion in the right Sunday suit? He is always left with the uneasy notion that maybe *any* objective drapery is as good as *any* other for any emotion. [. . .] Reluctantly, he comes to the conclusion that to account for his book is to account for his life, and he knows that that is impossible. [. . .]

So, at the outset, I say frankly that there are phases of *Native Son* which I shall make no attempt to account for. There are meanings in my book of which I was not aware until they literally spilled out upon the paper (pp. 1–2).

QUESTION: The title of your introduction, quoted here, is 'How "Bigger" was Born'. Is Bigger a part of you, or is this the story of a particular individual you have known? How much of the character of Bigger is drawn from your experience in your own life, and how much from observing the lives of others?

RW: The birth of Bigger Thomas goes back to my childhood, and there was not just one Bigger, but many of them, more than I could count and more than you suspect. But let me start with the first Bigger, whom I shall call Bigger No. 1.

When I was a bareheaded, barefoot kid in Jackson, Mississippi, there was a boy who terrorized me and all of the boys I played with. If we were playing games, he would saunter up and snatch from us our balls, bats, spinning tops, and marbles. We would stand around pouting, sniffling, trying to keep back our tears, begging for our playthings. But Bigger would refuse. We never demanded that he give them back; we were afraid, and Bigger was bad. We had seen him clout boys when he was angry and we did not want to run that risk. We never recovered our toys unless we flattered him and made him feel that he was superior to us. Then, perhaps, if he felt like it, he condescended, threw them at us and then gave each of us a swift kick into the bargain, just to make us feel his utter contempt. [. . .]

If I had known only one Bigger I would not have written *Native Son*. Let me call the next one Bigger No. 2; he was about seventeen and tougher than the first Bigger. Since I, too, had grown older, I was a little less afraid of him. And the hardness of this Bigger No. 2 was not directed toward me or the other Negroes, but toward the whites who ruled the South. He bought clothes and food on credit and would not pay for them. He lived in the dingy shacks of the white land-lords and refused to pay rent. Of course, he had no money, but neither did we. We did without the necessities of life and starved ourselves, but he never would. When we asked him why he acted as he did, he would tell us (as though we were little children in a kindergarten) that the white folks had every-thing and he had nothing. Further, he would tell us that we were fools not to get what we wanted while we were alive in this world. [. . .]

There was Bigger No. 3, whom the white folks called a 'bad nigger'. He carried his life in his hands in a literal fashion. I once worked as a ticket-taker in a Negro movie house [. . .] and many times Bigger No. 3 came to the door and gave my arm a hard pinch and walked into the theater. [. . .] 'Did he pay?' the proprietor would ask. 'No, sir,' I'd answer. The proprietor would pull down the corners of his lips and speak through his teeth: 'We'll kill that goddamn nigger one of these days.' And the episode would end right there. But later on Bigger No. 3 was killed during the days of Prohibition: while delivering liquor to a customer he was shot through the back by a white cop.

And then there was Bigger No. 4, whose only law was death. The Jim Crow laws of the South were not for him. But as he laughed and cursed and broke them, he knew that some day he'd have to pay for his freedom. [. . .] Bigger No. 4 was sent to an asylum for the insane.

Then there was Bigger No. 5, who always rode the Jim Crow streetcars without paying and sat wherever he pleased. [. . .] I don't know what happened to Bigger No. 5. But I can guess.

The Bigger Thomases were the only Negroes I know of who consistently violated the Jim Crow laws of the South and got away with it, at least for a sweet brief spell. Eventually, the whites who restricted their lives made them pay a terrible price. They were shot, hanged, maimed, lynched, and generally hounded until they were either dead or their spirits broken (pp. 2–5).

QUESTION: The novel documents a physical and economic separation between the black and white communities as well as a social and class-based division. Do you believe this still operates in the American consciousness? [Note: Wright wrote this in the 1950s. You must remind yourself that social conditions change, and bear in mind the particular historical context of his remarks.] What is the history of that separation?

RW: In Dixie there are two worlds, the white world and the black world, and they are physically separated. There are white schools and black schools, white churches and black churches, white businesses and black businesses, white graveyards, and, for all I know, a white God and a black God ...

This separation was accomplished after the Civil War by the terror of the Ku Klux Klan, which swept the newly freed Negro through arson, pillage, and death out of the United States Senate, the House of Representatives, the many state legislatures, and out of the public, social, and economic life of the South. The motive for this assault was simple and urgent. The imperialistic tug of history had torn the Negro from his African home and had placed him ironically upon the most fertile plantation areas of the South; and, when the Negro was freed, he outnumbered the whites in many of these fertile areas.

Hence, a fierce and bitter struggle took place to keep the ballot from the Negro, for had he had a chance to vote, he would have automatically controlled the richest lands of the South and with them the social, political, and economic destiny of a third of the Republic. Though the South is politically a part of America, the problem that faced her was peculiar and the struggle between the whites and the blacks after the Civil War was in essence a struggle for power, ranging over thirteen states and involving the lives of tens of millions of people.

[...] Had the Negro lived upon a common territory, separate from the bulk of the white population, this program of oppression might not have assumed such a brutal and violent form. But this war took place between people who were neighbors, whose homes adjoined, whose farms had common boundaries. Guns and disenfranchisement, therefore, were not enough to make the black neighbor keep his distance. The white neighbor decided to limit the amount of education his black neighbor could receive; decided to keep him off the police force and out of the local national guards; to segregate him residentially; to Jim Crow him in public places; to restrict his participation in the professions and jobs; and to built up a vast, dense ideology of racial superiority that would justify any act of violence taken against him to defend white dominance; and further, to condition him to hope for little and to receive that little without rebelling. [...] In the main, this delicately balanced state of affairs has not greatly altered since the Civil War, save in those parts of the South which have been industrialized or urbanized (pp. 5–7).

QUESTION: What inspired you to document this history of oppression and its continued role in American society? Did the Communist Party, or the 'labor movement' as you refer to it, play an important part in your decision?

RW: It was not until I went to live in Chicago that I first thought seriously of writing Bigger Thomas. Two items of my experience combined to make me aware of Bigger as a meaningful and prophetic symbol. First, being free of the daily pressure of the Dixie environment, I was able to come into possession of my own feelings. Second, my contact with the labor movement and its ideology made me see Bigger clearly and feel what he meant.

I made the discovery that Bigger Thomas was not black all the time; he was white, too, and there were literally millions of him, everywhere. The extension of my sense of the personality of Bigger was the pivot of my life; it altered the complexion of my existence. [...] Whenever I picked up a newspaper, I'd no longer feel that I was reading the doings of whites alone (Negroes are rarely mentioned in the press unless they've committed some crime!), but of a complex struggle for life going on in my country, a struggle in which I was involved. [...]

The urban environment of Chicago, affording a more stimulating life, made the Negro Bigger Thomases react more violently than even in the South. More than ever I began to see and understand the environmental factors which made for this extreme conduct. It was not that Chicago segregated Negroes more than the South, but that Chicago had more to offer (pp. 9–10).

QUESTION: Bigger is such a complex protagonist, at once sympathetic and horrifying, particularly in his treatment of Bessie, how did you go about constructing him?

RW: Let me give examples of how I began to develop the dim negative of Bigger. I met white writers who talked of their responses, who told me how whites reacted to this lurid American scene. And, as they talked, I'd translate what they said in terms of Bigger's life. But what was more important still, I read their novels. Here, for the first time, I found ways and techniques of gauging meaningfully the effects of American civilization upon the personalities of people. I took these techniques, these ways of seeing and feeling, and twisted them, bent them, adapted them, until they became *my* ways of apprehending the locked-in life of the Black Belt areas. This association with white writers was the life preserver of my hope to depict Negro life in fiction, for my race possessed no background in such sharp and critical testing of experience, no novels that went with a deep and fearless will down to the dark roots of life (p. 11).

So, with this much knowledge of myself and the world gained and known, why should I not try to work out on paper the problem of what will happen to Bigger? Why should I not, like a scientist in a laboratory, use my imagination and invent test-tube situations, place Bigger in them, and, following the guidance of my own hopes and fears, what I had learned and remembered, work out in fictional form an emotional statement and resolution of this problem (p. 16)?

First, there was his personal and private life, that intimate existence that is so difficult to snare and nail down in fiction,

that elusive core of being, that individual data of consciousness which in every man and woman is like that in no other.
I had to deal with Bigger's dreams, his fleeting, momentary
sensations, his yearning, visions, his deep emotional responses.
Then I was confronted with that part of him that was dual in
aspect, dim, wavering, that part of him which is so much a
part of *all* Negroes and *all* whites that I realized that I could
put it down upon paper only by feeling out its meaning first
within the confines of my own life (p. 19).

QUESTION: The novel is entitled *Native Son*. How does your
sense of Bigger's political exclusion relate to this title?

RW: I felt that Bigger, an American product, a native son of
this land, carried within him the potentialities of either
Communism or Fascism. I don't mean to say that the Negro
boy depicted in *Native Son* is either a Communist or a Fascist.
He is not either. But he is the product of a dislocated society;
he is a dispossessed and disinherited man; he is all of this, and
he lives amid the greatest possible plenty on earth and he is
looking and feeling for a way out. Whether he'll follow some
gaudy, hysterical leader who'll promise rashly to fill the void
for him, or whether he'll come to an understanding with the
millions of his kindred fellow workers under trade-union or
revolutionary guidance depends upon the future drifts of events
in America (p. 15).
    Bigger was attracted and repelled by the American scene.
He was an American, because he was a native son; but [...]
he was not allowed to live as an American. Such was his way
of life and mine; neither Bigger nor I resided fully in either
camp (p. 19).

QUESTION: Given the sensitive topics you tackle in the novel,
your treatment of rape, and the black man as criminal and

outcast, were you concerned that there would be a backlash from the black community you were apparently representing here?

RW: I asked myself: 'What will Negro doctors, lawyers, dentists, bankers, school teachers, social workers and business men, think of me if I draw such a picture of Bigger?' I knew from long and painful experience that the Negro middle and professional classes were the people of my own race who were more than others ashamed of Bigger and what he meant. Having narrowly escaped the Bigger Thomas reaction pattern themselves – indeed, still retaining traces of it within the confines of their own timid personalities – they would not relish being publicly reminded of the lowly, shameful depths of life above which they enjoyed their bourgeois lives. Never did they want people, especially *white* people, to think that their lives were so much touched by anything so dark and brutal as Bigger.

Their attitude toward life and art can be summed up in a single paragraph: 'But, Mr Wright, there are so many of us who are *not* like Bigger. Why don't you portray in your fiction the *best* traits of our race, something that will show the white people what we have done in *spite* of oppression? Don't represent anger and bitterness. Smile when a white person comes to you. Never let him feel that you are so small that what he had done to crush you has made you hate him! Oh, above all, save your *pride*!'

But Bigger won over all these claims; he won because I felt that I was hunting on the trail of more exciting and thrilling game. What Bigger meant had claimed me because I felt with all of my being that he was more important than what any person, white or black, would say or try to make of him, more important than any political analysis designed to explain or deny him, more important, even, than my own sense of fear, shame, and diffidence (pp. 18–19).

QUESTION: Which, if any, personal experiences have particularly informed this novel?

RW: The first event was my getting a job in the South Side Boy's Club, an institution which tried to reclaim the thousands of Negro Bigger Thomases from the dives and the alleys of the Black Belt. Here, on a vast scale, I had an opportunity to observe Bigger in all of his moods, actions, haunts. Here I felt for the first time that the rich folk who were paying my wages did not really give a good goddamn about Bigger, that their kindness was prompted at bottom by a selfish motive. They were paying me to distract Bigger with ping-pong, checkers, swimming, marbles, and baseball in order that he might not roam the streets and harm the valuable white property which adjoined the Black Belt. I am not condemning boys' clubs and ping-pong as such; but these little stopgaps were utterly inadequate to fill up the centuries-long chasm of emptiness which American civilization had created in these Biggers. I felt that I was doing a kind of dressed-up police work, and I hated it. [. . .]

The second event that spurred me to write of Bigger was more personal and subtle. I had written a book of short stories which was published under the title of *Uncle Tom's Children*. When the reviews of that book began to appear, I realized that I had made an awfully naïve mistake. I found that I had written a book which even bankers' daughters could read and weep over and feel good about. I swore to myself that if I wrote another book, no one would weep over it; that it would be so hard and deep that they would have to face it without the consolation of tears. It was this that made me get to work in dead earnest (pp. 22–3).

QUESTION: The novel itself sometimes disguises the craftsmanship of the author. Are there any sections you would describe as particularly contrived or constructed as fiction?

RW: There is a scene in *Native Son* where Bigger stands in a cell with a Negro preacher, Jan, Max, the State's Attorney, Mr Dalton, Mrs Dalton, Bigger's mother, his brother, his sister, Al, Gus, and Jack. While writing that scene, I knew that it was unlikely that so many people would ever be allowed to come into a murderer's cell. But I wanted those people in that cell to elicit a certain important emotional response from Bigger. And so the scene stood. I felt that what I wanted that scene to say to the reader was *more important than its surface reality or plausibility* (p. 27).

QUESTION: Equally, which elements of this novel have changed or developed in your rewrites?

RW: With the first draft down, I found that I could not end the book satisfactorily. In the first draft I had Bigger going smack to the electric chair; but I felt that two murders were enough for one novel. I cut the final scene and went back to worry about the beginning. I had no luck. The book was one-half finished, with the opening and closing scenes unwritten. Then, one night, in desperation – I hope I'm not disclosing the hidden secrets of my craft! – I sneaked out and got a bottle. With the help of it, I began to remember many things which I could not remember before. One of them was that Chicago was overrun with rats. I recalled that I'd seen many rats on the streets, that I'd heard and read of Negro children being bitten by rats in their beds. At first I rejected the idea of Bigger battling a rat in his room; I was afraid that the rat would 'hog' the scene. But the rat would not leave me; he presented himself in many attractive guises. So, cautioning myself to allow the rat scene to disclose *only* Bigger, his family, their little room, and their relationships, I let the rat walk in, and he did his stuff.

Many of the scenes were torn out as I reworked the book. The mere rereading of what I'd written made me think of the possibility of developing themes which had been only hinted at in the first draft. For example, the entire guilt theme that runs through *Native Son* was woven in *after* the first draft was written (pp. 29–30).

QUESTION: What do you perceive to be the fundamental difference between the 'author' and the 'reader'?

RW: Always, as I wrote, I was both reader and writer, both the conceiver of the action and the appreciator of it. I tried to write so that, in the same instant of time, the objective and subjective aspects of Bigger's life would be caught in a focus of prose. And always I tried to *render, depict*, not merely to tell the story. If a thing was cold, I tried to make the reader *feel* cold, and not just tell about it (p. 27).

I kept out of the story as much as possible, for I wanted the reader to feel that there was nothing between him and Bigger; that the story was a special *première* given in his own private theater (p. 28).

If I attempted to account for scenes and characters, to tell why certain scenes were written in certain ways, I'd be stretching facts in order to be pleasantly intelligible. All else in the book came from my feelings reacting upon the material, and any honest reader knows as much about the rest of what is in the book as I do; that is, if, as he reads, he is willing to let his emotions and imagination become as influenced by the materials as I did (p. 29).

HARPER LEE

Harper Lee is famous for her refusal to comment on her novel. When she received the Pulitzer Prize she declined to speak, and maintains an absolute silence about both her life as a writer and her relationship to *To Kill A Mockingbird*.

One of the central tenets of the *Vintage Living Texts* reading guides, however, is that the author should not be considered as the primary interpretative voice. We do not need to look to the writer to be instructed in the 'correct' reading of a novel. There are multiple 'readings' of novels, and – as long as each one can be justified by reference to the text – they can each be persuasive and provide a valid way into the text. For that reason, this introduction takes another approach to reading this novel.

In the London Folio edition of *To Kill a Mockingbird* (1996), Harper Lee allowed another author, Albert French, to introduce her work. He chose to do so with a story of his own. Brief quotations from that story are offered here, not only because they reinforce the idea that the author's reading is no more 'true' than that of any other readers, but also because French suggests that interpretation does not have to be a dry activity – it can be creative and dynamic – as his production of a story of his own suggests.

Identify from this story its themes, and consider how French's narrative parallels *To Kill a Mockingbird* itself. Look also at narrative style and tone. In what ways is it similar to Lee's novel?

I remember the time and the night well. There was a silence in my mind, deep in my mind. When I was talking with my mother, saying the things it was time to say, I could still feel the silence. There was fear lurking beneath the silence, my fear. I didn't want to tell Mom I was afraid, I couldn't. I was out of high school, too old to be afraid and tell Mom of my fears. I remember looking out the window and knowing the sun had lowered, the night would soon come. I knew the hours were few before it would be time to leave, go get on the train, go far away from home and my life as I knew it.

My sisters were very young, Sherri was only seven and Staci had just begun to walk. Throughout the evening I played with Staci, held her and told her things I knew she didn't understand. I had told her *your big brother's going to be a Marine*. I asked her if she was going to be a good girl while I was gone. She could only smile, maybe giggle, and touch my face with her little hands. Sherri was old enough to know I was going away and would not be back home for a long time. As I was packing, I tried to answer all her questions about the Marines and how long I would be away from home. I knew four years would be a long time, I didn't know I would be scarred and different forever when I returned.

I was an American, but I was afraid of America. I learned to be afraid of America when I was just a child living in my grandfather's house, even before I knew what was beyond the small house near the railroad tracks. Silent feelings came to me, seeped deep into my mind. I knew, felt, that there was something beyond the small house that would get me, make me cry. I didn't know what it was, but I was afraid of it. [. . .]

I was an American with a coloured face, a Negro, a nigger. I didn't want to be a nigger, didn't want that ugly feeling of not being allowed to do things and go places because I had a coloured face. I didn't want to change trains in Washington DC, get on the one that would take me to the South, down South, South Carolina, but the South had already come to me (p. 7).

I remember the feeling I had when the train crossed over the river that separates Washington DC from the State of Virginia and knew I had entered the South. I remember feeling so far away from home and even threatened by the pretty countryside the train was passing through. There were green hills with little patches of snow on them. Everything I could see out the train window seemed to be passing. The bright green hills became just long green blurs passing by the window. [. . .]

Years have passed since I took the train ride deep into the South. I was too young to know then, or even feel, that one day I would become a writer and write about the American South. I would write a novel called *Billy*, and another called *Holly*. Both about people coloured and white, their lives predetermined by a godless self-ordained order of evil. A racist order of evil, hundreds of years old once held together by the chains of slavery and written into the laws of the Southland. Maybe I saw the faces of my fictional characters along the tracks I travelled. Or maybe I didn't know that the train was only taking me back home to the land of my grandfather and mothers and I was already a part of everything I saw.

The spring and summer of my life have now gone by, I am fifty-two years old. I never knew the shadows of the South would still linger over America. Sometimes our cities still burn through the night while dark angry faces scream for justice in the light of the fires. A million black men have marched on Washington DC, showing their unity and opposition to the racist shadow that hovers over their lives. The crosses still burn and racism still haunts America. I am old now, it is the winter of 1996. I didn't know my life would be as it has been. I never thought I would be a writer and never knew that one day I would be asked to write of Harper Lee's *To Kill a Mockingbird*, see her characters rush back into my mind, realise they never left. *To Kill a Mockingbird* is a literary portrait of a small Southern town in the 1930s. The images and characters she creates will never fade from your mind. Her character, the white lawyer Atticus Finch, tries to defend a Negro and at the same time maintain his dignity when racism spits in his eye. His young daughter Scout will tell you why you should never kill a mockingbird, and you will never forget.

Although this is not an interview with Lee, you, the reader, are being directly addressed by an author. Use these questions to help you work with French's story:

- Does his attitude to the novel change yours, or if you have yet to read it, does he create any expectations about this text?
- How are you affected by how recently French wrote his narrative? Is it imporant to have a contemporary viewpoint on texts written some time ago?

In this way, by interrogating a text created – with the author's approval – about her text, you will be able to create your own 'interview' with the author, and reflect on the critical methods you use to make secondary texts into an analytical and critical tool.

J.D. SALINGER

If Harper Lee's silence is famous, then Salinger's is legendary. The lengths he goes to in order to keep his personal life private are clearly indicated in his professional and legal encounters with Ian Hamilton, who tried to publish a biography of Salinger. Salinger blocked the biography before it had even hit the shops. Not to be outdone, the resourceful Hamilton turned his encounters with Salinger – and his attempts to write his biography – into his own text, *In Search of J. D. Salinger*. In this account he gives a sense of just how determinedly reclusive Salinger is:

> I got a letter from J. D. Salinger himself. One of *my* letters, it seems, had been received by his sister, and another by his son, both of whom were listed in the Manhattan phone book. Salinger berated me for harassing his family 'in the not particularly fair name of scholarship'. He didn't suppose he could stop me writing a book about him, but he thought he ought to let me know – 'for whatever little it may be worth' – that he had suffered so many intrusions on his privacy that he could endure no more of it – not 'in a single lifetime'.

Hamilton demonstrates and exhibits Salinger's desire to be unknown by enumerating and ticketing all the many difficulties and trials he experienced in collecting information about the author.

> J. D. Salinger was born on January 1, 1919. His father, Sol Salinger, was born in Cleveland, Ohio, and is said to have been the son of a rabbi, but he drifted sufficiently far from Orthodox Judaism to become

an importer of hams and to marry a Gentile,
Scotch-born Marie Jillich, who changed her name to
Miriam to fit better with her husband's family.

This paragraph alone could take a year or two to
check. Where had these 'facts' come from?

Having established Salinger's refusal to enter into a public
debate about his life and his fiction, the following quotations
try to offer just a taste of the author's beliefs and concerns.
Each is given in context, to give you an idea of who the author
is talking about, and the character of his relationship to his
audience. The first quotation is – as Hamilton tells us –
'Salinger's only known public statement'. Here the author has
decided to speak publicly about prisoners in the New York
penal system, and, in particular, to consider the treatment of
people serving life sentences without parole:

This was surely 'justice-without-mercy' [. . .] the
bleakest, coldest combination of words in the
language. [. . .] Can it be brought to the attention of
the Governor? Can he be approached? Can he be
located? Surely it must concern him that the New
York State lifer is one of the most crossed-off, man-
forsaken men on earth.

In *In Search of J. D. Salinger* (1988) Hamilton goes on to
interpret Salinger's decision to speak out on this particular
issue. Here, however, as the author resists interpretation so
strongly, we are suggesting that you consider Salinger's statement in relation to the themes and issues discussed in *The
Catcher in the Rye*.

Frequently, Salinger comments, through his literature, on
the role of the author, and his or her relationship to the reading

public. This is the back cover to the 1963 edition of his text *Franny and Zooey* written by Salinger himself:

'Franny' came out in *The New Yorker* in 1955, and was swiftly followed, in 1957, by 'Zooey'. Both stories are early, critical entries in a narrative series I'm doing about a family of settlers in twentieth-century New York, the Glasses. It is a long-term project, patently an ambitious one, and there is a real-enough danger, I suppose, that sooner or later I'll bog down, perhaps disappear entirely in my own methods, locutions, and mannerisms. On the whole, though, I'm very hopeful. I love working on the Glass stories, I've been waiting for them most of my life, and I think I have fairly decent, monomaniacal plans to finish them with due care and all-available skill.

A couple of stories in the series besides 'Franny' and 'Zooey' have already been published in *The New Yorker*, and some new material is scheduled to appear there soon. I have a great deal of thoroughly unscheduled material on paper too, but I expect to be fussing with it, to use a popular trade term, for some time to come. ('Polishing' is another dandy word that comes to mind.) I work like greased lightning, myself, but my alter-ego and collaborator, Buddy Glass, is insufferably slow.

It is my rather subversive opinion that a writer's feelings of anonymity-obscurity are the second-most valuable property on loan to him during his working years. My wife has asked me to add, however, in a single explosion of candor, that I live in Westport with my dog.

In fact, this single detail, Salinger's home in Cornish New Hampshire, has tantalised biographers to such a degree that they will scale fences to see the inside of his house, or sit in cars in his town centre waiting for a glimpse of the author. On one occasion one of these critics did spot Salinger, but you will be unsurprised to discover that this sighting did not help the writer, Havemann, who observed, 'I don't know what Salinger was thinking.'

Salinger himself comments that he is grateful when his readers work out their reading with the text alone, leaving him outside of that interpretative act. This is his dedication in *Raise High the Roof Beam, Carpenters and Seymour, an Introduction*:

> If there is an amateur reader still left in the world –
> or anybody who just reads and runs – I ask him or
> her with untellable affection and gratitude, to split
> the dedication of this book four ways with my wife
> and children.

He speaks in much the same spirit about *The Catcher in the Rye* (reproduced in Hamilton's text), when he prematurely perceives it to be waning in popularity:

> The fact is, I feel tremendously relieved that the
> season for success of *The Catcher in the Rye* is over. I
> enjoyed a small part of it, but most of it I found
> hectic and professionally and personally demoralising.
> Let's say I'm getting good and sick of bumping into
> that blown-up photograph of my face on the back
> of the dust-jacket. I look forward to the day when I
> see it flapping against a lamp-post in a cold, wet,
> Lexington Avenue wind, in company with, say, the
> editorial page of the *Daily Mirror*.

Salinger goes as far, in *Raise High the Roof Beam*, as to suggest that criticism, even positive criticism, works to the detriment of the author: 'Yet the real artist, I've noticed, will survive anything. (Even praise, I happily suspect.)'

At this point, however, we have to return to Salinger's own warning. We should remember that this is a quotation from one of his stories, and absolutely not – as he is at pains to indicate – to be confused with, or interpreted as, an authorial statement from Salinger himself.

Perhaps the most interesting question for the contemporary reader is *why* the desire to know the author is so strong in this particular case. Harper Lee, herself a recluse, is not stalked by biographers, nor does she take out injunctions to safeguard herself against the more intrepid potential biographers. As always with *Vintage Living Texts*, the question is raised for you to consider.

As a starting point for your analysis, here is one possible reading of the desperate desire to know J. D. Salinger. Pamela Hunt Steinle explains in this paragraph that many readers read Holden Caulfield as if he were a real person:

> There is one unique participant whose 'voice' in this book bears some explanation. In J. D. Salinger's strategic choice to give the first-person voice to Holden Caulfield as the fictional narrator of the tale he also (and perhaps unwittingly) gave him a *fictional life*. From the earliest reviews by literary critics, to the responses of more general readership, to references in popular culture, Holden Caulfield is very often referred to as a real person. Hence, instead of discussing Holden as might be expected in a scholarly manuscript – as a fictional representation carrying out the author's narrative strategies as understood from the scholar's

perspective – I take my cue [. . .] and for the most
part address Holden Caulfield as someone alive.

One possible reading of the desire to know J. D. Salinger
is because we confuse Holden with Salinger. We want to know
the 'real person' behind the text, and if that is not Caulfield,
then it has to be Salinger – doesn't it? Certainly not, according
to the author of *The Catcher in the Rye*. Salinger's silence, therefore, is possibly less mysterious. He is aware of the separations
between author, text and reader, and – through his refusal to
comment on his novel – he maintains them.

JOSEPH HELLER

Joseph Heller died in December 1999. Unlike Harper Lee or
J. D. Salinger he had, at times, been willing to comment on his
work, and committed himself to a number of interviews in
different media. You can find some of these published interviews in Adam J. Sorkin, *Conversations with Joseph Heller*
(University Press of Mississippi, 1993).

As in the opening section on Richard Wright, this last section substitutes for an interview with Joseph Heller a reworking
of his own preface to the 1994 Vintage edition of *Catch-22*.
We have devised questions in relation to the stories that Heller
tells there, and provided answers which are his answers, bor-
rowed from that personal intervention. You can find Heller's
preface on pages 1–6 of the Vintage edition of *Catch-22*.

QUESTION: How and why did you start writing *Catch-22*?

JH: For me the history of *Catch-22* begins back in 1953, when
I started writing it. I was employed as a copywriter at a small

advertising agency in New York, after two years as an instructor in English composition at Pennsylvania State University. [. . .] Early on, in an anxious need of an approving opinion, I sent the opening chapter off to the literary agents I had managed to obtain after publishing a few short stories in magazines, in *Esquire* and *The Atlantic*. The agents were not impressed, but a young assistant there, Ms Candida Donadio, was, and she secured permission to submit a chapter to a few publications that regularly published excerpts from 'novels in progress'. [. . .] I was employed at *Time* magazine, writing advertising-sales presentations by day when not furtively putting thoughts down on paper for my work on the novel at home that evening (pp. 4–5 Vintage edition).

QUESTION: So the process of writing *Catch-22* and getting it out to the public was one that was essentially piecemeal, even collaborative?

JH: In 1957 when I had about 270 pages in typescript [. . .] Candida Donadio was establishing herself as a preeminent agent in her own right [. . .] We agreed it made sense to submit the partial manuscript to some publishers, mainly to obtain a practical idea of the potential for publication of the novel we both thought so much of. She was drawn toward a new young editor she knew of at Simon & Schuster, one she thought might prove more receptive to innovation than most. His name was Robert Gottlieb, and she was right.

While Gottlieb busied himself with those pages, I, with a four-week summer vacation from bountiful *Time* magazine, began rewriting them. Gottlieb and I met for lunch, mainly for him to gauge my temperament and ascertain how amenable I would be as an author to work with. After I listened to him allude with tact to certain broad suggestions he thought he might eventually be compelled to make, I handed him my new pages with the boastful response that I had already taken care of nearly all of them (p. 5).

QUESTION: What was the public reaction to the publication of *Catch-22*?

JH: Within days after publication, there was a review in *The Nation* by Nelson Algren [. . .] who wrote of *Catch-22* that it 'was the best novel to come out of anywhere in years'. And there was a review by Studs Terkel in a Chicago daily newspaper that recommended it about as highly [. . .] The work was not reviewed in the *Times* on publication. However, it was reviewed in the *Herald Tribune* by Maurice Dolbier, and Mr. Dolbier said of it: 'A wild, moving, shocking, hilarious, raging, exhilarating, giant roller-coaster of a book'.

That the reviewer for the *Herald Tribune* came to review at all this war novel by someone unknown was almost entirely the product of coincidence (pp. 1–2).

QUESTION: Was there any adverse reaction?

JH: The disparagements were frequently venomous. In the *Sunday Times*, in a notice in the back so slender that the only people seeing it were those awaiting it, the reviewer [. . .] decided that the 'novel gasps for want of craft and sensibility', 'is repetitious and monotonous', 'fails', 'is an emotional hodgepodge', and was no novel: and in the esteemed *The New Yorker*, the reviewer, a staff writer who normally writes about jazz, compared the book unfavourably with a novel of similar setting by Mitchell Goodman and decided that *Catch-22* 'doesn't even seem to have been written; instead, it gives the impression of having been shouted onto paper', 'what remains is a debris of sour jokes', and that in the end Heller 'wallows in his own laughter and finally drowns in it' (p. 3).

QUESTION: What was, or is, your reaction to this?

JH: I am tempted now to drown in laughter as I jot this down (p. 3).

QUESTION: How did readers react to the novel?

JH: Late that same summer [1962], I was invited to my first television interview. The program was the *Today* show, then a variety show as much as anything else. The interim host was John Chancellor. Mr Chancellor had recently returned from his newsman's post in the Kremlin, and he had agreed to accept the position on condition that he interview only those people he himself chose to.

After the show, in a bar close by the studio in which I found myself drinking martinis at an earlier hour than ever in my life, he handed me a packet of stickers he'd had printed privately. They read: YOSSARIAN LIVES. And he confided he'd been pasting these stickers secretly on the walls of the corridors and in the executive rest rooms of the NBC [National Broadcasting Corporation] building (pp. 3–4).

QUESTION: But why does Yossarian live in readers' minds? What does he represent for them?

JH: On February 28, 1962, the journalist Richard Starnes published a column of unrestrained praise in his newspaper, *The New York World-Telegram*, that opened with these words: 'Yossarian will, I think, live a very long time.'

[. . .] Yossarian has indeed lived a long time. Mr Starnes has passed on. Many people mentioned in that first advertisement [endorsing the novel at its first publication in November 1961] have died, and most of the rest of us are on the way.

But Yossarian is alive when the novel ends. Because of the

motion picture [made in 1970, directed by Mike Nichols], even close readers of the novel have a final, lasting image of him at sea, paddling toward freedom in a yellow inflated lifeboat. In the book he doesn't get that far; but he is not captured and he isn't dead (p. 6).

QUESTION: So where is Yossarian now?

JH: At the end of the successor volume I've just completed [in 1994], *Closing Time* [. . .] he is again still alive, more than forty years older but definitely still there. 'Everyone has got to go,' his physician friend in that novel reminds him with emphasis, 'Everyone!' But should I ever write another sequel, he would still be around at the end.

Sooner or later, I must concede, Yossarian, now seventy, will have to pass away too. But it won't be by my hand (p. 6).

Three different types of authorial silence are examined here; they have different causes and different explanations, but they share one feature. They highlight the importance of the reader in the job of interpretation and, in their different ways, show that there is no such thing – for any text – as one 'authorised' reading.

VINTAGE
LIVING
TEXTS

Native Son

IN CLOSE-UP

Reading activities: detailed analysis

BOOK ONE: FEAR
SECTION 1 (pp. 33–42)

Focus on: language

FRAME . . .

— If you have studied the introduction you will be aware of
Richard Wright's desire to communicate particular ideas in this
novel. (If you have not read the 'interviews and silences' section
in this text it is important that you read it. Notice that the novel
is preceded by Wright's introduction – 'How "Bigger" was born'
starts on page 1, the novel begins on page 33.) As well as being
clear about his thematic intentions, Wright also employs various
literary devices. Use this first section to think about how the
novel's narrative construction reinforces its thematic concerns.

DEFINE . . .

— In order to think about these narrative constructions first
define them. This section opens with an extended metaphor.
What is a 'metaphor'? How is it different from a 'simile'? Use
the glossary if necessary. When you are clear about 'metaphor',
use the resources you are provided with here to think about
what an *extended* metaphor is.

EXAMINE . . .

— The novel opens with Bigger's family starting their day in
the cramped apartment they share. Much of the action is taken
up with Bigger's hunting of a rat (pp. 34–9). Work your way
closely through the passage examining the novel's treatment of
the rat. What is happening to it? Who is the aggressor? Do
we sympathise with the rat? Do we know whether it has any
feelings? Why does Wright choose a rat? Is it an animal we
have positive associations with? What ideas do we associate
with rats? Think closely about the rat's treatment, how it is
hunted and trapped.

EXPLORE . . .

— The rat is often critically represented as an extended
metaphor for Bigger. Using your definition of the term and
your analysis of the text, explore the employment of this
extended metaphor.
— Think carefully about the model you have constructed for
the rat:

● What expectations are created for the plot when you consider the rat as being Bigger?
● What themes are established here?
● How does it alter your attitude to Bigger – he is not only
  the killer of the rat, but also the rat itself?

— When you have thought about the extended metaphor,
analyse Wright's decision to open the novel with this incident.
Why does he choose to open his text with a hunted rat? (You
may want to discuss this, comparing your attitudes to rats and
the associations you have made, with other readers, students
or colleagues.)
— As you work your way through the text, come back to the
idea of the rat – do rats reappear at any point in the novel,

extending the metaphor beyond this opening section?
— How are your expectations met by the action of the novel?
— Can you use this metaphor as shorthand for the novel's plot and themes?

BOOK ONE: FEAR
SECTION 2 (pp. 42–57)

Focus on: power

DETAIL AND RESEARCH . . .
— Work your way carefully through the section picking out the different power relationships you encounter here. Remember to consider both the people Bigger encounters and his role play with Gus. Make sure that you understand the specific references made. So, for example, if you are not sure of the difference between the army ranks mentioned, or who J. P. Morgan is, find out (with the help of your teacher or group leader) to clarify the particular powers being invoked.

CATEGORISE . . .
— When you have teased out the different kinds of power the text employs, draw up categories to differentiate between the forms of power you encounter here. For example, which forms of power do the characters have and which do they fantasise about? Separate 'actual' power from 'fantasy'. What categories do the characters employ – what do they regard as 'white' power?

INTERROGATE . . .
— Look at the distinctions you have made in your analysis of these categories. What similarities do you note between the characters' understanding of 'white' power and your understanding of 'fantasy' here?

— Why do you think the text so clearly differentiates between the actual power these characters have and the opportunities they perceive as only being available to others?

DISCUSS . . .

— Think about the association of the power of the criminal with Bigger and his friends. How is their power unacceptable, or illegitimate – do we regard it as an abuse of 'proper' power? Talk through the idea presented: that 'white' power is connected with authority, and 'black' power with an abuse of power – through violence and criminality. (You may wish to discuss contemporary events in the light of this novel, but for a fuller discussion of criminality see the Contexts section for this novel on pp. 84–6.)

— Also discuss the relationship between 'fear' and 'power' here. How does fear reinforce Bigger's feeling of power? Is he himself scared? As you continue your analysis, bear in mind the relationship between fear and power – why, for example, does Wright decide to call this opening section 'Fear'?

BOOK ONE: FEAR
SECTION 3 (pp. 57–73)

Focus on: Cinema

LIST AND ANALYSE . . .

— Focus on the treatment of Bigger and Jack's trip to the cinema (pp. 57–64). There are two films being shown – one 'white', one 'black'. Draw up a list of what differentiates the two films. Remember to bear in mind the following questions:

● What do their titles signify?
● What are you told about the plots of the two films – what

kinds of assumptions do you make about them on that basis?

● How are characters described – what differences do you note in the treatment of them?

ESTABLISH . . .

— When you have looked at the text's treatment of the different films, establish how they are juxtaposed. What contrasts are highlighted between 'white' and 'black' culture here?

— Having thought about the differences established here, think about why the villain in the 'white' film is a *'Communist'* (p. 62).

— Use the suggestions in the Contexts section on pp. 86–7 as well as your teacher or group leader to establish an understanding of Communism. Its key figures include Marx, Engels and Gramsci, but you may prefer to focus your examination on its central beliefs. How does Communism understand religion? What is its attitude to class? Does it regard the aristocracy as sacred?

LINK . . .

— When you have formed a basic understanding of the central tenets of Communism, return to the question of why the villain in the film is a Communist. What is it that frightens the characters in the film – what class are the characters? Are they the same social group as the audience? (The American attitude to Communism is discussed in more depth in the Contexts Section for this novel on pp. 86–7, and you could include your responses to that here.)

— Think about how the text uses films to set up particular ideas about 'whiteness' 'blackness' and 'Communism' here.

BOOK ONE: FEAR
SECTION 4 (pp. 73–93)

Focus on: blindness

DETAIL . . .

— 'He looked round the room; it was lit by dim lights glowing from a hidden source. He tried to find them by roving his eyes, but could not' (p. 76). Work your way through the section, looking closely at Wright's employment of sight. Pick out the particular words and phrases, such as the one above, where sight is used to suggest perception. Bigger cannot see the lights here, but he is also unable to *perceive* where light is coming from.

DEVELOP . . .

— Use your close analysis of the text to think about different kinds of 'seeing' – what is the difference between sight and perception, for example? How is the idea of 'blindness' used to suggest emotional and psychological as well as physical lack of sight?

DISCUSS . . .

— Get together and talk about the establishment of blindness at this point. What is the effect of Wright making Mrs Dalton blind? What is sight used to signify here? How does it establish themes for the novel as a whole?

EXTEND . . .

— When you have discussed the treatment of sight here, you may want to extend your analysis to consider the relationship of sight to colour. What does it mean to be 'colour blind'? How does the text play on the idea of being sightless, or short-sighted, as both a positive and a negative construct?

— Blindness is a central thematic concern within the novel. As you work your way through the text, return to the question of blindness and the conflicts it embodies. Keep coming back to the following questions:

- How does Mrs Dalton's blindness alter our attitude to the events of the novel?
- Which characters are blind – Mrs Dalton, Bigger, Bessie?

BOOK ONE: FEAR
SECTION 5 (pp. 93–112)

Focus on: dialogue

TRANSFORM AND PERFORM . . .
In this section Bigger encounters Jan for the first time. The section begins with his conversations with Mary and features his interpretation of what she says and how she speaks to him (pp. 93–6). Jan then joins them and Bigger is involved in a conversation that alienates him.

— Treat this section of text as a piece of script – read the dialogue aloud, leaving out the descriptions and internal narration Bigger gives you.

— When you have read through the scene, think about the particular use of language in the dialogue you have performed. How do characters refer to one another? Is it a form of conversation you are used to hearing – if not, why not? How does the text read differently when you ignore the context that the narrator gives you? Do you understand the dialogue differently?

REINTRODUCE . . .
— Having thought carefully about the use of dialogue here,

turn your attention to the narration that forms the context for the conversation you have performed. What specific information are you given about characters and their attitudes? How are misunderstandings spelled out by the narrator, or how is Bigger's position clear from the dialogue itself?

— Concentrate upon the relationship of dialogue to the character of Bigger and how we, as readers, come to understand how uncomfortable he feels. Do we sympathise with him when we look solely at the dialogue? How does overhearing a direct conversation create intimacy? Does it make the reader feel more involved to 'overhear' rather than to have a conversation reported by the narrator?

— Remember to focus your attention here on the relationship of dialogue to the narrator and think about how direct speech affects the reader.

BOOK ONE: FEAR
SECTION 6 (pp. 112–25)

Focus on: plot

SELECT . . .

— This section is the climax of the first book of the novel: it contains the events that motivate the text as a whole. Read through the section selecting only the events that occur here. What actually happens? What actions do the different characters take?

COMPARE AND CONTRAST . . .

— It may be useful to compare your versions of the events narrated here with those of other readers. What subtle differences do you note? Use the following questions to help you interrogate the variations in your accounts:

- What word have you chosen to describe Mary's death –
  'murder', 'accident', 'death', 'struggle'?
- Did you include Mary's drunkenness in your account?
- How detailed is your version of Bigger escorting her to
  bed?
- Which details did you consider to be important that some-
  body else had overlooked?
- How fully do you refer to the disposal of the body?

— Through these comparisons think about how these details
characterise a *different* story.

INTERPRET . . .
— The next two books within the novel hinge upon the events
narrated here. Think about how selective this account is. Does
the reader *know* what actually happened – was Mary murdered?
Spend some time considering how the novel establishes this
crucial complexity. You are taken through the events as though
you were a witness, but your knowledge is limited; as a result,
what choices are you forced to make about Bigger?
— Think about how these choices affect your interpretation
of the text as a whole. Do you decide his 'guilt' at this point?
Think about how the novel complicates categorising Bigger by
apparently giving us total access to what occurs. Does a detailed
account of the facts make absolute knowledge simpler?

BOOK TWO: FLIGHT
SECTION 1 (pp. 127–41)

Focus on: flight

DESCRIBE . . .
— 'He wished that he could rise up through the ceiling and

float away from this room, forever' (pp. 132). Focusing on this opening section of Book Two, and including the title, describe the different references to flight given here. Where and how does it feature? (Remember to include both direct and indirect references.) Also think about what kind of verb 'to fly' is – is it always active, or is it sometimes passive? Is it aggressive – do you associate it with the idea of a criminal or a victim?

CONSIDER . . .

— Look over your descriptions and think about the different ways in which flight is employed here. In some ways it fits with Book One – flight can also mean 'escape'. But consider also the ways in which its usage is surprising – 'flights of fancy', for example, seem to overtake Bigger.

— Use your consideration of this particular term to think about what concerns it sets up for Book Two. Does it establish Bigger as a criminal? Does it isolate the reader from him or is it used to re-establish your sympathy for him after the brutality of Book One's ending? Also consider how these expectations are carried over to Book Two as a whole – why is this book entitled 'Flight'?

BOOK TWO: FLIGHT
SECTION 2 (pp. 141–51)

Focus on: emotions

DISTINGUISH . . .

— 'It was not Mary he was reacting to when he felt that fear and shame. Mary had served to set off his emotions, emotions conditioned by many Marys' (p. 144). Pick out the various emotions traced by the narrator in this section. Here, alone, Bigger refers to two. Sort the differing emotions you note into categories and think about what distinguishes 'fear and shame' (p. 144) from 'guilt' (p. 149).

CHARACTERISE . . .
— Look over the variety of emotions you have identified here. Consider how the complexity of Bigger's state of mind is suggested by so many different kinds of emotion. How are they juxtaposed? How do you form an understanding of Bigger's state of mind by examining the conflicting emotions the narrator identifies?

COMPLICATE . . .
— What emotions characterise Bigger for you at this point? Do you consider him to be predominantly frightened, or excited? Would you want to choose an emotion not directly referred to in the text, such as 'exhilarated', or 'overwhelmed'?
— As you make your choices think about how difficult it is to determine complicated emotions textually. Do you have to use conflicting emotions to suggest the tension operating within Bigger? Does the use of many different emotions give Bigger psychological complexity for the reader? If so, how?
— Return to your discussion of his emotional state, and your attitude to it, as you work your way through the novel. You may want to return to this exercise as you analyse Bigger's treatment in court – think about how simple other characters believe him to be, and how this is undermined throughout the narrative.

BOOK TWO: FLIGHT
SECTION 3 (pp. 151–9)

Focus on: alcohol

DISCOVER . . .

Both Mary's family, and Bigger himself, consider her drunkenness to be an important factor in her disappearance. They all suggest that it indicates serious flaws in her character, 'She was *drunk*, I tell you. I never thought she'd come home in that condition' (p. 155).

— All the characters regard this as an important piece of information. With the help of your group leader or teacher, find out what prevailing attitudes to alcohol were in America in the 1930s. What is 'prohibition'? What is 'moonshine'? What does 'bootlegging' mean?

— When you are carrying out research into the period as a whole, focus particularly on what it means for a woman to be drunk in this period. Why is alcohol particularly socially unacceptable in terms of female consumption – how is it 'unladylike'?

— Also, bear in mind the relationship between alcohol and vulnerability. Think of examples (from books, films and personal experience) where drunkenness makes people, but particularly women, vulnerable.

REINTERPRET . . .

— When you have found out more about the period's attitude to alcohol, and particularly to women drinking, look again at this passage. Given your developed understanding, consider why Wright chooses to make Mary drunk. How does it influence your attitude to Bigger when you consider how unacceptable Mary's behaviour is, in terms of the moral codes operating when the book was written?

RETURN . . .

— The question of Mary's drunkenness is central to the novel's treatment of race. Reconsider its importance when you have focused upon race and white fears of the 'black man'. Think about what Mary's drunkenness means for this debate.

BOOK TWO: FLIGHT
SECTION 4 (pp. 159–79)

Focus on: the character of Bessie

CHARACTERISE . . .

— Although references are made to Bessie throughout the novel, and she appears briefly when Bigger takes Mary and Jan for chicken, this is the reader's first real encounter with Bessie. Use this section of text to construct a character analysis of Bessie. Pay attention to Bigger's version of her, but be careful to distinguish between his character analysis and your own. How does Bessie *resist* Bigger's version of her?

INCORPORATE . . .

— When you have constructed a character analysis of Bessie that allows for the differences between Bigger's interpretation and your own, think about how Bessie fits in the novel as a whole.

— Why does Wright decide to introduce us to Bessie – what function does she perform for the novel? (Remember to think thematically as well as in terms of the plot.) Which characters is she set up to parallel and contrast?

— Return to your responses to these questions as you read on. How does your perception of Bessie change in the light of the novel's development? Keep a note of how your attitudes alter – what impression are you left with at the end of the novel? Is it constant with your conception of her here?

BOOK TWO: FLIGHT
SECTION 5 (pp. 179–93)

Focus on: genre

ANALYSE AND INTERPRET . . .
— This section opens with Bigger's attempts to cover up Mary's death and then the reader is introduced to Britten, the detective (p. 184). The introduction of the detective opens a new phase to the novel as the hunt for Mary sets in motion the hunt for her killer. Take this particular change of focus to examine what kind of novel you would categorise *Native Son* as – which genre would you place it in? Use the list below to determine what genre of novel best describes *Native Son* for you.

- Murder mystery
- Slave narrative
- Horror
- Communist manifesto
- Detective story
- Love story
- Biography
- Autobiography

— You may find that none of the categories suggested fit your version of this novel's genre, in which case, add your own choices to the list. Equally, if you do not understand any of the terms, use the glossary, the Contexts section on pp. 81–7, and your teacher or group leader to determine exactly what they mean.

— If you have categorised the novel, what has led you to select the term you have chosen? Either cite evidence from the text from this section, or you could broaden your analysis to include evidence from other areas of the novel.

REVISE . . .

— As you work your way through the novel, look back over your preferred choice of genre. Is it still the most appropriate of the terms offered? For example, would you categorise Book Three as a 'detective story', or would you choose another genre?

— Look over the development between the different choices you have made, think about how they affect your understanding of the novel, and how you would use your choice of genre to communicate the novel's thematic concerns to someone else.

BOOK TWO: FLIGHT
SECTION 6 (pp. 193–204)

Focus on: narrative voice

EXAMINE AND INTERROGATE . . .

— 'Britten was familiar to him; he had met a thousand Brittens in his life. [. . .] Should he try to get money from them now? Hell, yes! He would show that Britten bastard!' (pp. 193–4). Focus on narrative voice in this section. The above quotation is an example of the close relationship between the novel's protagonist, Bigger, and the narrator. At one point in this example it seems that Bigger is speaking, but the speech is not put in speech marks. Therefore, it is not separated from the voice of the narrator.

— Examine the complex treatment of narrative voice in this novel, and use the following questions as a means of interrogating the text.

- How many narrators do you encounter in this section of the novel?
- Is Bigger a narrator?
- Is the narrator named here?
- What is the relationship between Bigger and the various narrators – is this, in fact, ever made clear?

— As you examine the narrative voice, try to establish whose voice is predominant. (You may want to look back over 'Interviews and silences', and particularly at Wright's discussion of constructing Bigger on pp. 15–17 and pp. 20–2. Be very wary of treating the author and the narrator as one voice.) Think about your relationship with the narrator – do you trust the narrator, or do you read his narration sceptically?

REFLECT . . .

— Having made your relationship to the narrator a conscious one, think about how this affects your reading. Have you already questioned the relationship between the narrator and Bigger, or the narrator and the author? Has your analysis of the narrative voice and the extent to which it blends with Bigger disrupted your reading of the novel? Are you less trusting of the agenda of the narrator, or has thinking consciously about its role made you recognise the extent to which you agree with him/her?

BOOK TWO: FLIGHT
SECTION 7 (pp. 204–14)

Focus on: settings

MAP AND TRACE . . .

— Throughout this section, specific references are made to

the city in which the novel is set. Establish which city that is and find a map of it. Trace out the different locations Bigger refers to. Think about how locating a narrative in an actual city suggests that it is a 'real', or true, story.

RELATE . . .
— Much of the novel focuses upon how Bigger is excluded, socially and economically, as well as on the grounds of colour. Think about the geography of your home. How are you excluded from certain areas of your locality? It may be because you live isolated from other homes and have to travel to visit neighbours. Or it might be that you live in a city and certain areas are off-limits because your family believe them to be dangerous. What is your attitude to those places? Does it make you particularly keen to travel to them, or are you suspicious of them?
— Think about settings in which you feel, or have felt, conspicuous. What was it about that particular setting that made you feel uncomfortable? Do your feelings about that setting in any way parallel Bigger's – have you ever felt unwelcome, or that you are being watched?

PARALLEL . . .
— Take your observations about your own experiences and think about Bigger's attitude to the city and its various spaces. Do you behave differently when a certain location puts specific pressures on you? How does being aware that you are 'in the wrong place' affect your behaviour? How does your translation of Bigger's treatment into your own experience affect your attitude to Bigger?

BOOK TWO: FLIGHT
SECTION 8 (pp. 214–24)

Focus on: Communism

REVISE . . .

— If you completed the exercise on 'cinema' (on p. 46–7 of this guide) you may have already conducted some research into Communism. However, this is an opportunity to extend that analysis. Look over your notes and refresh your memory before you embark on this exercise so that you do not duplicate material.

RESEARCH AND CONTEXTUALISE . . .

— 'The "Red" he had signed the letter and the hammer and curving knife would make them look for Communists' (p. 218). This sentence alone presumes a certain amount of knowledge about Communism and its symbols. In order to understand the references made, research the following topics.

- Who was Karl Marx, and how did his philosophy set up a 'Communist Ideology'?
- What are the central tenets of Communism? (Which ideas are most popularly associated with it? You might like to try typing 'communism' into an Internet search engine and seeing what responses you get.)
- Which country, or countries, are predominantly associated with Communism?
- What do you understand the attitude of Americans to be to to Communism? (Be careful not to confuse decades – although anti-Communist feeling was an important feature of the 1950s and 1960s, Wright's novel pre-dates these historical facts.)

APPLY . . .
— As the novel develops the idea of Communism as a threat
to America's status quo, the treatment of Communists is dealt
with in more detail. At this point use your knowledge to
inform your reading of the novel's treatment of both Jan and
Bigger as 'suspects'. Bigger is excluded on the grounds of
colour, Jan because of his political beliefs. Why, as Wright
suggests through Bigger and Jan, are these political beliefs so
threatening?

BOOK TWO: FLIGHT
SECTION 9 (pp. 224–40)

Focus on: Guilt

RESEARCH AND CLARIFY . . .
'He knew that whites thought that all Negroes yearned for
white women, therefore he wanted to show a certain fearful
deference even when one's name was mentioned in his presence' (p. 227). This notion, the idea that the ultimate object of
desire for the black man is a white woman, is a central myth
in American culture. Novels such as James Fenimore Cooper's
The Last of the Mohicans (1826), Margaret Mitchell's *Gone With
the Wind* (1936), even, in fact, Puritan settler narratives such as
Anne Bradstreet's account of her arrival in America, deal with
the prospect of the white woman's rape.
— While tackling the text it is important to clarify black masculinity as a stereotype. Construct a working definition, either
by researching the topic or discussing within a group. You
might refer to images of masculinity in *The Oxford Companion
to African American Literature* or to Hazel Carby's *Race Men*,
which questions twentieth-century black male archetypes. (You
can also find a fuller discussion of the role of the rape and

its treatment in American culture in the Contexts sections on pp. 84–6.)

— Make sure that you are clear that black masculinity is not being used here in terms of 'sexual *desire*'. Rather, it is employed here as an 'idea', or a possibility, which frightens the white population – the fear of black masculinity as physical force and power. Have you come across this stereotype before? (You might want to think about how it has changed in contemporary culture.)

IDENTIFY . . .

— This idea, the black man ravishing the white woman, informs much of the novel. Throughout this section Bigger is trying to set Jan up to detract attention from himself. Look closely at the language here and pick out examples that suggest Bigger's knowledge of the stereotypes they are applying to him. How are his answers informed by what he knows of American myths about the black man?

EXTEND . . .

— As you work your way through the novel come back to these stereotypes and think about how they are employed. Which characters invoke them? Who repudiates them? (In order to develop your understanding of black masculinity as it is represented here, and its relation to rape, see the Contexts section entitled 'Rape' on pp. 84–6.)

Focus on: the press

DETAIL . . .

— The second part of this section focuses upon the press's treatment of Mary's disappearance (pp. 232–40). Pay particular attention to the relationship of the press to the treatment of the 'crime' being investigated. How does the text suggest the importance of representation through the role of the press here? Why are 'excerpts' from newspaper accounts included within the novel?

TRANSFORM . . .

— Write an article setting out your version of events as they have been presented to you as a reader. What is your headline? Look over your 'report' and think about the selective nature of the press. Also write a brief commentary on how your article has represented the events.

QUESTION . . .

— Interrogate the role of the media in this novel. Is the text offering a critique of the press? Does Wright use the press to highlight particular versions of communities – the black community or the Communists, for example? Think about the role of the press as you understand it – you may want to look at particularly famous media treatments of crime such as the cases of O. J. Simpson, Fred and Rosemary West, or Myra Hindley. Use the Internet to look at press treatments of these people. What shorthands are employed? How are these individuals represented? What stereotypes are employed, and to what effects?

— Use these examinations to think about the role of the press in the novel, and how Bigger is represented by it in *Native Son*.

BOOK TWO: FLIGHT
SECTION 10 (pp. 240–54)

Focus on: autonomy

DEFINE . . .

— Work in groups to produce a definition of 'autonomy'. Consider the following questions:

- Is it the same as being an individual?
- Are we all autonomous? Which members of society do we not recognise as being autonomous?
- Think about laws that 'protect' those who are not autonomous. At what age do we become 'autonomous'?

ANALYSE . . .

— Now turn your attention to the section of text and look at how Bigger plays with the idea of autonomy. Do the press regard him as an autonomous individual? If not, pick specific examples that explain how they regard him. How does the idea that he lacks autonomy work in his favour at this point in the novel?

— Also consider how this lack of autonomy is fundamentally a problem for Bigger. Come back to this notion as you work your way through the novel. How has society's refusal to recognise Bigger's autonomy led to the position he finds himself in?

BOOK TWO: FLIGHT
SECTION 11 (pp. 254-72)

Focus on: object versus subject

EXAMINE . . .

— This part of the text deals with Bessie's murder. Unlike Mary's death the text is unequivocal about Bigger's desire to kill Bessie. Focus on Bessie's treatment in this section, looking primarily at whether she is a 'subject' or an 'object'. (If you are not sure about the terms, use the glossary to help you.) Pick out the phrases used to describe her. Do they establish her individuality, or is she treated as an obstacle in Bigger's path?

— As part of your analysis, remember to think about the treatment of her as a 'body'. Think about her as a sexual, as well as a physical, object. Does Bigger desire her as a person, or as an object? How does he behave towards her as a body once he has killed her? Does he show any remorse — if so, what for, and how does it affect your interpretation of Bessie?

EXPLORE . . .

— The idea of female identity as being 'object' to the male 'subject' is crucial to feminist thought. If you are interested in exploring the binary of object versus subject in relation to 'man' versus 'woman', you may want to look at *Literary Theory: An Introduction* (1998), and its collection entitled 'Feminism'. This includes essays by Luce Irigaray and Hélène Cixous. Or read Deborah Cameron's text, *Feminism and Linguistic Theory* (1992), which sets out the relationship of feminist politics to language.

BOOK TWO: FLIGHT
SECTION 12 (pp. 272–84)

Focus on: appetite

DETAIL . . .

— Select and list the different references to appetite at this point in the novel. Also look closely at each instance and keep the following issues in mind: whose appetite is it? Is it being satisfied? Is it controlled?

EXTEND . . .

— This novel frequently uses the body as a metaphor. Think about the treatment of appetite – is it a sophisticated craving (champagne and caviar), or is it basic (bread and water)? What does Bigger's appetite tell us about him as a character? How does it suggest his humanity?

— When you have considered how his appetite characterises Bigger, make sure that you have thought about different kinds of appetite besides hunger. What other appetites do you recognise – sexual, social, career? How is appetite linked to capacity? What does it mean to be insatiable?

— You may also want to consider whether or not communities can have appetites. Is the desire to capture Bigger an appetite for revenge?

— Consider the notion of 'appetite', literal and metaphorical, in the text as a whole. (You could go back and look at the meal Jan, Bigger and Mary share.)

BOOK TWO: FLIGHT
SECTION 13 (pp. 284–301)

Focus on: hunting

ANALYSE . . .

— 'The one fact to remember was that eight thousand men, white men, with guns and gas, were out there in the night looking for him' (p. 287). The novel focuses here upon the police hunt of Bigger. Pick out the different references to hunting here, and think about its use as a metaphor – what specific phrases and descriptions highlight Bigger's arrest as a hunt?

PARALLEL . . .

— The novel builds upon various hunts: the hunt of an animal – the rat that is hunted and killed at the opening of the novel; the idea of a police hunt; the historic hunt of escaped slaves. Choose one of the forms of hunt given here and find out more about how it introduces particular thematic concerns. For example, if you select the idea of the animal being hunted, think about your attitude to that animal – how sympathy is constructed – and compare the language of the opening to the language of this section. If, however, you choose the idea of the slave hunt, compare the narrative to stories such as Harriet Beecher Stowe's *Uncle Tom's Cabin* (1852) or Harriet Jacobs's *Incidents in the Life of a Slave Girl* (1861). How is Bigger treated as 'property', or an object? Here, Bigger is a villain – how does the story's paralleling of slave narratives complicate this idea, and does the parallel suggest that he is also a hero?

REINTERPRET . . .

— Work together and tease out the different hunting narratives you have investigated and paralleled. How do they alter your perception of the novel at this point? Does introducing other narratives complicate your attitude to Bigger at this point?

BOOK THREE: FATE
SECTION I (pp. 303–11)

Focus on: threes

CONSIDER . . .

— Take a moment to think about the novel as a whole, and its division into three sections. 'Threes' are significant in Western culture and narratives. Think about popular culture, myth and fairy stories. How does the number three commonly operate? You could consider Goldilocks, the Three Little Pigs, Cinderella or the phrase 'third time lucky'. How does the structure of three operate in these narratives? What expectation do readers have for the third section, or character, in a fairy story?

COMPLICATE . . .

— When you have considered how three acts as a model in popular culture, think about how the opening of this final section subverts those expectations. How does Bigger's position undermine the positive associations three has for contemporary readers?

EXTEND . . .

— Having considered how *Native Son* complicates common associations with a three-part narrative structure, ponder how three operates in other ways in our culture. You may, for example, want to focus on religion: what, in terms of the Christian faith, is the 'Holy Trinity'? In a three-part cultural construction where would you locate Bigger at the opening of this third section: heaven, earth (or purgatory) or hell?

— How else is three culturally significant? Talk through your ideas, and remember to link them back to the novel. Can you determine how they operate to influence your reading or expectations?

BOOK THREE: FATE
SECTION 2 (pp. 311–23)

Focus on: Christianity

CLARIFY . . .

'They were silent. The wooden cross hung next to the skin of Bigger's chest. He was feeling the words of the preacher, feeling that life was flesh nailed to the world, a longing spirit imprisoned in the days of the earth' (p. 316).

— This section of the novel is predominantly concerned with Bigger's conversation with the preacher. Before looking at the text itself, work together to establish an understanding of Christianity. Start by mapping out the basics. Who are its major figures? What is its sacred text? What significantly differentiates it from Judaism, Buddhism or the Muslim faith?

— Work as a group or class to establish what 'Christian values' are. What do you understand the main tenets of the faith to be?

INTERROGATE . . .

— When you have established a set of values for Christianity, turn your attention back to the text, and pick out the particular words and phrases in which you find those values reflected in the text.

— Would you want to describe Bigger as a Christian?

— It has been argued that Bigger is himself a Christlike figure. To what extent do you agree with this version of him? (Remember to justify your response with evidence from the text.)

69

BOOK THREE: FATE
SECTION 3 (pp. 323–340)

Focus on: naturalism

CONSTRUCT . . .

— Using the resources provided here and with the help of a glossary or your teacher, construct a definition of naturalism as a literary term. You may want to draw on your understanding of art, television and film, but make sure your definition is then focused on the idea of writing naturalistically. Also, make sure that your definition includes examples that clarify your understanding. You might like to look up 'Naturalism' in the *Oxford English Dictionary*. How does it suggest meaning through examples? Try and take your examples from the novel itself.

ASSESS . . .

— Look at Richard Wright's introduction to this novel. How does his version of naturalism fit with your definition? On pp. 26–7 he discusses in particular detail the section of text you are focusing on here. Do you agree with his assessment of naturalism and the points at which it has to be rejected?

— Now turn your attention back to the section highlighted. Using your definition and Wright's introduction, question the extent to which it is anti-naturalist. Would you describe the novel as a whole as naturalistic, except for this one section? If not, would you regard naturalism as an inappropriate category for this novel? How would you prefer to categorise it?

BOOK THREE: FATE
SECTION 4 (pp. 340–58)

Focus on: inquests

RESEARCH . . .

— Bigger is led to the inquest. Use the textual evidence you are provided with here and, with your own research, develop an understanding of the term 'inquest'. As a starting point try to answer the following questions:

- What is an inquest?
- How is it different from a trial?
- What is a coroner attempting to establish – is it the same thing as a judge attempts to establish?
- Can a coroner pass sentence?
- Does an inquest have a jury; if so, what is its function?
- What is an inquest trying to establish?

DISCUSS . . .

— When you have developed an understanding of the process of an inquest, talk through why the text focuses so closely on the inquest. Think about how the text arouses sympathy. Also, consider the concerns of the inquest and their differences from a trial – how does Wright use these differences to privilege certain conversations? (You may want to combine your analysis of this section with the discussion of 'evidence' that follows in the next section.)

BOOK THREE: FATE
SECTION 5 (pp. 358–69)

Focus on: evidence

ASSESS AND QUESTION . . .

— 'As Deputy Coroner, I have decided, in the interests of justice, to offer in evidence the raped and mutilated body of one
Bessie Mears' (p. 359). Assess the decision to introduce Bessie
as a piece of evidence. Think about what evidence is – is the
coroner interested in her murder in its own right, or is it evidence of something else? Bear in mind:

- The treatment of her as an object here. (You may want to
  look back to Sections 4 and 11 of Book Two and your
  analysis of Bessie's treatment as an object throughout the
  novel such as you were asked to make on p. 65 of this
  guide.)
- The reaction of the crowd. Is the text making an argument about sensationalism here? Is Bessie's body shown
  as evidence or used an emotive device?
- The nature of facts. What evidence does Bessie's body
  actually provide? How is it interpreted by the coroner's
  court? How important is the interpretation of the fact of
  her body here?

— You may want to turn your responses into an essay – 'What
is a body of evidence?' How does the text undermine the idea
that facts are simple, straightforward and resist interpretation?

BOOK THREE: FATE
SECTION 6 (pp. 369–92)

Focus on: communication versus isolation

UNRAVEL AND DESCRIBE . . .

— 'He would not mind dying now if he could only find out what this meant, what he was in relation to all the others that lived, and the earth upon which he stood' (p. 392). Take time to tease out the text's treatment of 'communication' and 'isolation'. Break this section up into three parts: look at the man Bigger shares a cell with (pp. 372–4); at Bigger's prolonged conversation with Max (pp. 374–88); and Bigger's processing of the conversation (pp. 388–92).

— These three sections develop an argument about the relationship of isolation to Bigger's predicament. They also suggest that meaningful communication is the only way to overcome that separation. Pick out the particular elements of each part that highlight communication, and how it undermines each individual's isolation.

— Using the evidence you have taken from the text, construct a description of the arguments the text makes through Max and the 'nuts' cellmate (p. 374). Imagine that you are describing to someone who has not read the novel the argument that convinces Bigger that he has been 'blind' (p. 392).

BOOK THREE: FATE
SECTION 7 (pp. 392–410)

Focus on: naming

LIST . . .

— List the different names used to describe Bigger in this section. For example, he is described as 'the Negro' (p. 395), 'boy' (p. 400), 'the defendant' (p. 404). Keep a note of the exact context of the reference – are particular adjectives used to qualify the naming, such as 'sadistic Negro' (p. 410)?

DEVELOP . . .

— Look over your list and think about how particular names are applied because of their associations. Jot down what the resonances of particular terms are – what do you associate with 'boy'? What does describing someone as a 'Negro' suggest to you?

— Think about your development of the name associations. Use it to develop an argument about the role of naming in the construction of Bigger's identification as the rapist and murderer.

— You may want to take this discussion a stage further and think about the importance of naming in relation to the construction of identity. How does Bigger's naming literally fix his identity here? What does it mean to be labelled as a killer, or as having committed 'black crimes' (p. 404). (You may want to link your responses to this section with the final section of the text.)

BOOK THREE: FATE
SECTION 8 (pp. 410–30)

Focus on: polemic

DEFINE . . .
— Use the glossary to define 'polemic'. What is it as a form of communication? Who do you commonly expect to communicate using polemic? Is it often employed as a narrative device?

IDENTIFY . . .
— Look over Max's defence of Bigger. Think about how it is constructed – who is Max talking to? How many audiences can you identify for this speech? Pick out examples of phrases or sentences that you think characterise his speech.

CATEGORISE . . .
— Using the textual evidence you have chosen, as well as your answers to the questions suggested, categorise Max's address. Either pick from the list below, or come up with a term you believe describes this section of text.

- Polemic
- Rhetoric
- Storytelling
- Personal account
- Testimony
- Narrative
- Memory

COMPARE AND TALK THROUGH . . .
— In a group or class, compare your choices. Form a collective list, vote on the terms you believe should be used, having debated each choice and the reasons you would fight

for it to be included or rejected. Do you agree on any single defining term? If not, why not? Are there some contradictions in your choices – can something be both a personal account and rhetorical? How are these contradictions productive?

BOOK THREE: FATE
SECTION 9 (pp. 430–42)

Focus on: language

ANALYSE AND INTERPRET . . .

— Focus on the use of italics in this section. What are italics? What is their purpose? How are they correctly used? (Consult a dictionary if you are unsure.)

— When you are clear about their literary function, think about the following questions:

- Why does the author choose to italicise certain parts of the text?
- What do they emphasise?
- Do you read italics differently to the body of the text?

PLAY . . .

— You might want to write out the italicised words separately from the rest of the section. Consider how you might interpret them differently when the words are isolated from the text that surrounds them. Do they give you a shorthand account of what this section of text is preoccupied with?

— Why, for example, is the word 'worse' italicised in the sentence 'Your Honor, must not this infernal monster have burned her body to destroy evidence of offenses *worse* than rape?' (p. 436). How is the meaning of the sentence changed if you shift the italics?

REFLECT . . .
— Think about the function of italics and how they are applied here to reinforce particular meanings. How are italics used to control interpretation?

BOOK THREE: FATE
SECTION 10 (pp. 442–54)

Focus on: the death penalty

DEBATE . . .
— The novel closes with Bigger on death row. Set up a formal debate as a group. Before you start your discussion, have a vote – who supports the death penalty, and for which crimes? – and note the results. Then appoint a chairperson and choose people to argue the case for and against the death penalty. Try and draw evidence from the text to support your side of the argument. However, also inform your debate by reference to other examples, be they narrative or historical.
— When each side has presented its case, open questions to the group as a whole, arbitrated by the chair. Close your discussion with a second vote. Has anyone changed his or her position as a result of your debate?
— When the debate is concluded, spend some time talking about whether or not your attitude to the death penalty has been affected by the novel. If so, be clear about the effect the novel has had.

Focus on: identity

DETAIL AND CHARACTERISE . . .
— Read the closing section carefully and detail the change in

Bigger's self-perception. How has his view of himself altered as a result of his contact with Max? How does Bigger now perceive his identity in relation to his crimes?
— When you have characterised Bigger's understanding of himself, contrast it with Max's reaction to that understanding – why, for example, are his eyes 'full of terror' (p. 453)?

EXPLORE . . .
— The text explores the idea that identity is constructed by society's assumptions about the individual. The assertion that black men want to rape white women actually 'creates' Bigger as a rapist and murderer. It is his 'fate' (p. 454). Think about this version of identity. Do you support the idea that the racial stereotypes applied to Bigger actually construct his identity?
— Take both this section and the novel as a whole and consider the construction of Bigger's identity as unavoidable, or fated. You may want to bring in both the Contexts section pp. 81–7 and the 'Interviews and silences' pp. 14–25 to support your argument.

Looking over the whole novel

QUESTIONS FOR DISCUSSION OR ESSAYS
1. To what extent would you define this novel as 'polemic', and do you find that the novel's style effectively communicates its thematic concerns?

2. Choose one character from the novel and discuss how his or her characterisation is shaped by the text's Communist agenda – how are they constructed in relation to Communism?

3. How does Native Son employ extended metaphors to underline the main action of the novel?

4.   Compare and contrast the two treatments of rape in this novel. Why does Wright include two rapes, and what is highlighted by their juxtaposition?

5.   To what extent does 'How "Bigger" was Born' offer an explanation for the novel itself? What areas of the text do you feel are left unaccounted for? If you could ask Wright questions based on this introduction, what would they be?

6.   'What I killed for must've been good!' (p. 453). Imagine you are describing this novel to a friend. How would you characterise Bigger's killings, and to what extent does your attitude to them dominate your understanding of the novel?

7.   Look at the novel's treatment of colour. How does Wright complicate ideas about colour through his treatment of vision and blindness?

8.   Analyse the novel's treatment of different forms of writing. Why, for example, does Wright include 'excerpts' from newspapers?

9.   What are some of the real historical events that are alluded to – directly or indirectly – in *Native Son*, and what effects does Wright create by weaving them into his text?

Contexts, comparisons and complementary readings

These sections suggest contextual and comparative ways of reading the four novels in this volume. Here, the focus is Richard Wright and *Native Son*. You can put your reading in a social, historical or literary context. You can make comparisons – again, social, literary or historical – with other texts or art works. Or you can choose complementary works (of whatever kind) – that is, art works, literary works, social reportage or facts which in some way illuminate the text, by giving a framework to references you currently find oblique. Some of the suggested contexts are directly connected to the book, in that they will give you precise literary or social frames in which to situate the novel. In turn, these are either related to the period within which the novel is set, or to the time – now – when you are reading it. Some of these examples are designed to suggest books or other texts that may make useful sources for comparison (or for complementary purposes) when you are reading *Native Son*. Again, they may be related to literary or critical themes, or they may be relevant to social and cultural themes current 'then' or 'now'.

The first two contexts for Wright raise identical concerns to those tackled in relation to Harper Lee. This is important, as the novels share not only their historical context (although they were published twenty years apart), but also their thematic concerns – the possibility of rape, and its relationship to representations of black masculinity, means that these contexts are relevant to both novels.

Focus on: the history and legacy of slavery

RESEARCH . . .

— *Native Son* is predicated upon the history of slavery. Look back over the 'interview' with Richard Wright, paying attention to his discussion of the reception of his first novel, *Uncle Tom's Children* (1938). Throughout his essay 'How "Bigger" was Born', and within the novel as a whole, Wright makes clear the relationship between slavery and segregation – the result of the Civil War and the particular American versions of black identity current when the novel was written.

— Using the bibliography, as well as the Internet and libraries to which you have access, create a working knowledge of the historical context of the novel. You will find the 'American Memory' website at the Library of Congress useful. Below is a list of key terms – use them as a means of beginning your investigation by discovering what these terms mean.

- Chattel
- Negro
- Emancipation
- Abolitionists
- Civil War
- Segregation
- Fugitive Slave Laws
- Ku Klux Klan

— When you are clear about these specific terms, extend your research. Think about what it means to demarcate identities along colour lines. Through your research you will also have come across some discussion of the consequences of segregation — what it means to be allowed to sit in only one part of a bus, or to be forced to use a different toilet to the white community. This will be developed later in the contextualisation, but bear in mind the value judgements being instituted here.

— Next, look into the following phrases, the historical keynotes that mark our understanding of the slave trade, and the history of segregation it has established. What specific identifications, events and practices do they refer to?

- Institution of slavery
- One-Drop Rule
- Dixie
- Jim Crow
- Nigger

— Find out when segregation was formally ended in the United States — does how recent the date is shock you?

COMPARE . . .

— Compare Wright's novel, which was said to have a profound effect on understanding the oppression of the black community, with other seminal texts. Harriet Beecher Stowe's novel, *Uncle Tom's Cabin*, is said to have inspired Lincoln to support emancipation, which led to the American Civil War. Look at her treatment of black identity. Bear in mind that this text was the inspiration for Wright's *Uncle Tom's Children*, and that the response of white readers to this novel disgusted him.

— You may want to compare Wright's treatment of the history of the black community with Harper Lee's novel. Both texts focus on the same period – are they informed by a similar understanding of the history and legacy of slavery? How do these accounts temper your response to *Native Son*?

Focus on: rape

ESTABLISH . . .

This *Vintage Living Text* acknowledges the brutal reality of rape statistics in the United Kingdom.

- 1 in 4 women will suffer rape or attempted rape at some point in their lifetime.
- The most common rapists are current and ex-husbands or current and ex-partners.
- 1 in 7 married women say they have been forced to have sex, compared to 1 in 3 divorced or separated women.
- 91 per cent of women tell no one.

Source: Kate Painter (1991)
www.rapecrisis.co.uk/statistics.htm 17/10/02

— Notice that in the context of *Native Son*, rape is employed as a political and cultural act, as well as the violent sexual act Bigger perpetrates on Bessie. The novel itself is unconcerned with Bessie, the courts are not interested in her welfare, the compassionate Communists barely refer to it. The central act of 'rape' in this narrative is Bigger's supposed attack upon Mary, which you, the reader, are fully aware did not occur.

DISCOVER . . .

— The idea of rape is important in both a literary and a historical context. Look over the list below and bear in mind its historical scope.

- The Greek Legend *Tereus and Philomela*
- *The Rape of Lucrece* (William Shakespeare)
- *Titus Andronicus* (William Shakespeare)
- *The Rape of the Lock* (Alexander Pope)
- *Charlotte Temple* (Susanna Rowson)
- 'Leda and the Swan' (W. B. Yeats)
- *Gone with the Wind* (Margaret Mitchell)
- *To Kill a Mockingbird* (Harper Lee)
- 'Act of Union' (Seamus Heaney)

— This list is deliberately disparate — it covers many centuries, includes writers from more than one country, and features plays, poems and novels. You may want to read one of the titles — some are parodies, some do not even refer to human individuals, but employ rape, instead, in the context of one nation's relationship with another or as a metaphor for other kinds of assault.

— The particular importance of these texts is that 'rape' here is not necessarily a literal act. Often the rape itself does not take place, but the fear of it dominates the text. Look closely at its treatment as a metaphor here, and establish what rape means as a metaphor. What sort of power relationship does it represent?

HISTORICISE . . .

— When you have established 'rape' as a metaphor, its particular context in American culture is your next focus. The 'fantasy', or 'fear' of black masculinity has been a central cultural concern, which was established during America's period of slavery and reinforced after the Civil War. In order to appreciate this history, look at Toni Morrison's *Playing in the Dark: Whiteness and the Literary Imagination* (1992); *Race-ing Justice, En-gendering Power: Essays on Anita Hill, Clarence Thomas, and the Construction of Social Reality* (1993); and co-written and edited with Claudia Lacour, *Birth of a Nation 'hood': Gaze, Script and Spectacle in the O. J. Simpson Case* (1997).

— Through your historicisation you are forming an understanding of the centrality of 'rape fantasy' to American culture. You have examined it in its literary form and come to know something of its historical background. To what extent has this deepened understanding altered your attitude to *Native Son*?

Focus on: Communism

RESEARCH . . .

— Communism is a complex political and moral ideology. It is important for this novel that you understand its basic premises, as these ideas underpin Wright's novel. He cites the importance of Communism, or 'the Communist Party', at length in his essay 'How "Bigger" was Born' (p. 17). Use the following breakdown as a starting point for your analysis, and draw upon library and Internet resources to help you with your research.

Symbols	What is the association between 'red' and Communist?
	What is the hammer and sickle Bigger refers to?
Figures	Who are Marx, Engels, Lenin, Gorky? Why are they famous?
Ideas	What is Marxism?
	What is the Communist attitude to religion?
	How do Communists perceive class distinctions?
History	Which parts of the globe do we associate with Communism? Trace out America's attitude to Communism over the last century. Remember to pinpoint the history in relation to *Native Son*; do not confuse 1950s attitudes to Communism with its reception in the 1930s.

LINK . . .

— Take your, now more sophisticated, understanding of Communism and focus your attention back on the text itself. How does your heightened knowledge change your attitude to the characters of Max and Jan? What effect does it have on your perception of Bigger? Does it widen the gap between Bigger and Wright? Does this novel read as a political manifesto in support of Communism?

Focus on: Film adaptations

COMPARE MEDIA . . .

— *Native Son* has been adapted twice for the cinema. In 1950 Pierre Chenal directed a low-budget adaptation which is mainly interesting because Wright himself plays Bigger Thomas. In 1986 Gerrold Freedman directed another version that compresses the event and excises large sections of the text. If you can see this version, consider how the modifications alter Wright's novel. How successfully does the novel transfer to the screen?

To Kill a
Mockingbird

IN CLOSE-UP

Reading activities: detailed analysis

PART ONE

CHAPTER 1
(pp. 3–16)

Focus on: time

EXAMINE . . .
— Look at the initial chapter and think about the passage of time in this novel. At what point in the action does the novel open? Is the story entirely in the present tense? What role, if any, does the future play? How important is the past to this story?

IDENTIFY . . .
— When you have considered these relatively general questions, think about how you would characterise the style of narrative. Use the list below to stimulate your analysis. (If you feel the suggestions don't fit your definition, introduce your own.)

● History
● Story
● Biography

- Autobiography
- Retrospective

— Take evidence from the text to support your choice, and remember to consider both narrative style and the employment of time. Do you want to use more than one term? Is it both a history and a biography?

COMPARE AND CONTRAST . . .
— When you have made your choice, compare the narrative style to other narratives written in a similar mode. For example, Charlotte Brontë's *Jane Eyre* (1847) is also an adult's account of the protagonist's past. Look particularly at sections of the novel where Jane is writing in the present tense about her own childhood, and think about how it parallels Scout as she narrates her own history as if it is still in process. If you have regarded the text as predominantly a history, you could look at the parallels between this text and William Faulkner's *Absalom, Absalom!* (1936), which traces the history of a family in the Southern states, and deals with the history of slavery for the region. You could compare and contrast these novels' treatment of the history of the South. Begin by comparing their opening chapters, but you may wish to extend your analysis and look at the novels in their entirety.

CHAPTER 2
(pp. 17–24)

Focus on: education

RESEARCH . . .
— This chapter deals with Scout's first encounter with school. Discover something about the education system being parodied

here. What, for example, is the 'Dewey Decimal System'? (p. 20). Find out what you can about the 'new' system within the novel.

DEVELOP . . .

— When you have researched this education system, look at the chapter's treatment of this system. How does the text set up a critique of the system indirectly? In what ways does it suggest that the system defines knowledge too narrowly? How are other forms of learning denigrated or undermined here?

DISCUSS . . .

— When you have examined the chapter's treatment of forms of education, consider the novel's position. Do you think the academic education that preoccupies Miss Caroline is still the one we privilege? What other forms of education are respected in our society? Do you agree with this text that a practical knowledge of the world we inhabit is a sophisticated form of understanding? It is not presented here as a lesser form of education than an academic one.

— You may also want to discuss who has access to education, as well as the privileging of certain types of learning. Which communities are apparently absent from the school?

CHAPTER 3
(pp. 25–35)

Focus on: class

DISTINGUISH . . .

— When Scout takes Walter home for lunch, the reader is made aware of the importance of class distinction and social order. Pick out the parts of the text that clearly divide the children from one another through class. In this social hierarchy who exists at the highest level? Are Walter Cunningham and Burris Ewell from the same social class? If not, how is this made clear to the reader? How does Atticus explain to Scout that she must attend school by drawing on class distinctions?

DISCOVER . . .

— Social hierarchy plays a crucial role in this novel; the hierarchy is clearly in place and is invoked throughout the text as justification for both crimes and their punishment. The distinctions are subtle but absolute, as Atticus's discussion with Scout suggests. One particular group is drawn in this chapter that is fundamental to the novel's social structure. The Ewells are 'white trash'. Discover what this term means. Be specific in your definition – it is a particularly southern-American term, and has a particular meaning. What behaviour is expected from white trash? What is the relationship between the black community and white trash?

BEAR IN MIND . . .

— When you are confident about the term, think carefully about its relationship to the social structure of the novel. The idea of a clear and fixed distinction, appreciated by both the white and black communities, has important consequences for the novel. You may want to re-evaluate your treatment of 'white trash' as the novel develops. How is the community employed to maintain the hierarchy that places the white community as socially superior to the black community?

CHAPTER 4
(pp. 36–45)

Focus on: myths versus fairy stories

CLARIFY . . .

— "'Yawl hush,'" growled Jem, "you act like you believe in Hot Steams'" (p. 41). Work your way through this chapter focusing on the myths that operate here. Think about the function of myths. What do we mean when we call something an 'urban myth'? How many myths do you identify in this part of the novel?

— When you have teased out these particular myths, think about what categorises them as myths. What are the differences between myths and fairy stories? We tend to associate fairy stories with children; does that mean that the narratives of the three child protagonists at this point are fairy stories? Sketch out the differences as you perceive them and then re-examine the stories produced here. Is Boo's narrative, for example, a myth or a fairy story?

EXPAND . . .

— When you have considered the differences between myths and fairy stories think about the function of myth in this narrative. Jot down some ideas as to why Lee sets up the myth of the Radley property. How are myths employed culturally here? What do you regard the functions of myths to be?

— Keep coming back to your ideas about why cultures employ myths. How do your explanations alter as you work your way through the novel?

CHAPTER 5
(pp. 46–55)

Focus on: the character of Miss Maudie

CHARACTERISE . . .

— The novel introduces the reader to Miss Maudie in this chapter. Use it to construct a character analysis of Miss Maudie. Start with the basics – what can you establish about the facts of her life, her age, looks and situation from the text? Then move on to other facets of her character. How much are you told of her history? How is she characterised in terms of nature, emotion and morality? What is her religious code? How does she provide a context for other characters?

ANALYSE . . .

— When you have drawn on the textual evidence about Miss Maudie in this chapter, stop and analyse the kinds of information you are given. Use the following questions as starting points for considering Miss Maudie's function within the novel.

- What important familial role does Miss Maudie supply for the protagonists?
- What is her position in the community of Maycomb? For whom does she act as a mouthpiece?
- How does the information she provides you with here change your attitude to other characters?

COMPLICATE . . .

— Take your responses to the questions suggested above and complicate your answers. Think about *why* Lee feels the need to create Miss Maudie. What is she a mouthpiece for? How is she used to present an alternate viewpoint to those of the children?

Why does Lee go to such lengths to establish her as a respectable and likeable character?

— By complicating your analysis of Miss Maudie, think about the novel's development and how she aids it. Pay particular attention to her discussion with the children. What political and moral viewpoints does Miss Maudie represent at this point in the novel? As your analysis progresses, come back to your examination and think about how crucial this position is to the novel's thematic and political concerns.

Focus on: boundaries

CONSIDER AND EVALUATE . . .

— Look at the second section of this chapter (pp. 51–5) and focus on the use of boundaries. How do Jem and Dill force boundaries on Scout? How are they transgressed? Look particularly at the challenges the boys make in terms of boundaries. How are physical boundaries used here to mirror personal and moral ones?

— Think about the nature of crossing forbidden boundaries and their relationship to growing up. Come up with examples, either personal or fictional, whereby the idea of maturing is suggested by crossing boundaries. To what extent is adulthood about being able to cross boundaries and thus assert our individuality?

CHAPTER 6
(pp. 55–64)

Focus on: narrative style

DETAIL . . .

— Look at the journeys the characters take in this chapter. Detail them and analyse the different forms of journey. For example, the chapter is predominantly concerned with Jem's attempt to see Boo (p. 57), but other characters make important movements – Atticus, and Boo himself, for example.

— Remember to consider different kinds of journey – as well as physical, literal forms of travel, journeys can be emotional, philosophical, moral and spiritual. Think about how you would characterise the different journeys you have identified.

CONSIDER THE QUEST . . .

— When you have detailed the different kinds of journeys embarked on here, think about your understanding of journeys in relation to literature. The quest narrative, the protagonist (traditionally male) searching for a goal – be it a wife, treasure, philosophical truth – is one of our culture's central storytelling modes.

— Spend a few minutes noting down as many different quest narratives as you can. Include fairy stories and myths, as well as famous novels, plays and films. Then consider how many different kinds of journey they represent.

EXPLORE . . .

— Use this consideration of the central nature of the quest narrative to our culture to think about the structure of this form of story. Map out its pattern. What is the usual plot formation? What kinds of characters does it demand? What twists of plot, or obstacles, do you regard as being part of the model? How does it end? What kinds of changes do you expect from the protagonists?

— Take your model and think about its application in terms of this chapter. How does Jem's narrative fit your expectations for the quest narrative? In what ways is the narrative subverted?

— You may want to extend your analysis to consider the novel as a whole, so return to your model when you have worked your way through the text. Could it be described as a quest narrative? How is the model complicated in this text? How does Lee employ our expectations – does she challenge them or work within them?

CHAPTER 7
(pp. 64–70)

Focus on: narrative perspective

TRANSFORM AND ALTER . . .
— This chapter focuses upon Boo's gifts to Jem and Scout. Take this chapter and rewrite it from the perspective of Boo. This may sound like a relatively straightforward task, but in order to give Boo's narrative you will need to set the story differently in terms of time and location. You will also have to change the active and passive. In the text the gifts are actively received but appear out of nowhere; an individual does not actively present them. In your version the action of giving will be active but the receipt of the presents will not necessarily be witnessed by Boo himself.

EVALUATE . . .
— When you have completed your rewrite, consider how it shifts the narrative's attention. How is suspense altered? How is sympathy created? Atticus famously warns Scout, 'You never really understand a person until you consider things from his point of view [. . .] until you climb into his skin and walk around in it' (p. 33). Think here about how important narrative perspective is. Simply by shifting narrator the story is not different but a new story.
— Think about the employment of perspective as you continue your analysis. The novel shifts narrative voice at important moments. Consider the consequences of these shifts. How is the story framed by these changes?

99

CHAPTER 8
(pp. 70–82)

Focus on: settings

CONTEXTUALISE . . .

— The novel is very specifically located in Maycomb, Alabama. Try to find out as much as you can about the context of the novel's location. Maycomb was modelled on Monroeville, Alabama. Use the Internet to find out about this town, which has its own website. This chapter focuses upon the unusual weather, the snow. Find out if this gives you a date for the novel – did it snow in Alabama in the 1930s? Is snow unusual, in fact? Does the climate described fit with your research? Where is Alabama? What is the name of the state capital?

— In order to research the context fully, locate Alabama historically as well as geographically. (You may want to allocate a question to each student and then to pool your resources, or you might wish to research the topic more thoroughly as a group.) Use the following questions as a starting point:

- Which side was Alabama on in the Civil War?
- What values was that side fighting for?
- What is Alabama's historical attitude to slavery?
- What can you discover about Alabama in the 1930s – is it famous for being a racially tolerant or intolerant state?
- Was segregation practised in Alabama – if so, what is segregation?

— Equally, use the textual information you are provided with about the geographical and historical location of the novel (look both forwards and backwards in time for details that provide context) in its particular place in American history.

INTERROGATE . . .

— When you have finished contextualising the novel's historical and geographical setting, think about why so much specific information is provided. What special importance is afforded to the location when it is described in such detail? Does it make the novel appear more 'realistic' – if so, *how*? What is it about the contextual detail that gives the novel this authority?

— Think also about how your research has changed your attitude to the text. What has surprised you in your research? Be specific about how knowing more about the novel's context has altered your reading. You may want to talk through those changes – has anything struck you as a group? Think about why that might be the case – what contextual knowledge changes your attitude as a reading community?

CHAPTER 9
(pp. 82–98)

Focus on: representation

ASSESS . . .

— Pay particular attention to the beginning and end of this section (pp. 82–5 and 93–8). Tease out the various levels of representation that concern the novel here. For example, Atticus represents people as a 'lawyer', but he is also conscious of less literal forms of representation. Work your way through these sections selecting the various treatments of representation. What do you consider representing someone else to mean? How is it different from standing up for yourself as an individual? Look at the discussion of Scout's fight with Francis (pp. 93–6). How are views represented here?

EXPAND . . .

— Atticus discusses representation through naming, and is careful to correct Scout: "'Do you defend niggers, Atticus?'" [. . .] "Of course I do. Don't say nigger, Scout'" (p. 83).

— So far you have considered representation as a professional activity, and the ways in which an individual represents their own views. Now turn your attention to the relationship of representation to naming and communities. Much of the attention here focuses on the representation of the black community.

— Think about the different names that are used to describe a community you identify with, and how the name you choose alters your understanding of that community. For example, the difference between naming someone 'Christian' and 'God squad' gives a different understanding of that community.

— Consider how important naming is in terms of representing communities. Think about how this section of the novel deals with the question of naming, and the relationship between an individual viewpoint and the representation of a community.

Focus on: Christmas

LIST . . .

— Work as a group to draw up a list of the *values* you associate with Christmas. Rather than jotting down 'turkey' and 'ivy', think about what you consider Christmas celebrates spiritually and morally, such as generosity and charity. Establish what you understand its religious values to be. To what extent are these values specifically Christian?

INVESTIGATE AND DETERMINE . . .

— When you have completed your analysis of *To Kill a Mockingbird*, look over the novel as a whole and consider whether or not the Christian values you identified as informing the spirit of Christmas, can be applied to the text as a whole.

Is the moral code this book argues for a 'Christian' one? Remember to back up your argument, whether you support or reject this idea, with evidence from the novel.

CHAPTER 10
(pp. 98–109)

Focus on: belonging versus not belonging

ANALYSE . . .
— Scout is unconvinced by her father's judgement when she witnesses his shooting of the 'mad dog' (pp. 106–7). Think about the treatment of belonging to a community here. How is Atticus confirmed as a member of the community of Maycomb? Look particularly at the mad dog: how does he function as a metaphor for Atticus as Scout perceives him?
— Consider how belonging is defined by the binary of outsider/insider. You establish yourself as belonging to a community by demonstrating that you fit certain criteria, setting yourself against an outsider or someone who does *not* belong.
— What are the criteria established in this chapter for belonging to the community of Maycomb? Look particularly at Atticus, the mad dog (pp. 105–9) and the mockingbird (pp. 99–100). How is cruelty employed as a standard for measuring the nature of 'belonging'?

QUALIFY . . .
— When you have considered the role of cruelty in establishing membership to this community, think about how this is qualified in the text. How is cruelty justified and redefined, for example, in relation to both Atticus and the children in their use of guns?
— Think about how the simple belonging/not belonging

binary slips depending upon who defines the terms. The 'outsiders', presumably the bluejays and the dog, it could be argued are being treated cruelly. Would that not make the Finch family outsiders?

— Spend some time thinking about this slippage. How is belonging determined by hierarchy? Who has the power to decide who belongs in this community? How is this power explained and arbitrated?

CHAPTER II
(pp. 110–24)

Focus on: bravery

DEFINE . . .

— Come up with a definition of 'bravery'. How do you characterise it? Cite examples both personal and literary, and where possible use the text to provide you with evidence.

— As part of your definition, consider whether or not you would characterise bravery in terms of gender. Do you think of bravery as a primarily masculine form of behaviour? If you do consider it to be masculine, then justify your reading. Equally, if you reject the idea of it as a male quality, then support and clarify this argument. Would you argue that it is, in fact, a primarily feminine characteristic?

APPLY . . .

— Take your definition and apply it to this chapter. Does your definition of bravery match Atticus's? (p. 124). If not, how does Mrs Dubose complicate your definition? Would you want to rework your definition in relation to the chapter? If not, how would you argue against this version of bravery?

QUESTION . . .

— Reflect upon why the text includes this didactic episode. In what ways does this chapter influence the rest of the novel, in terms of plot, characters and themes? Why is Mrs Dubose an important character? What impact does she have upon the novel's plot? Is she used to establish a set of values? Or is she used implicitly to criticise other characters? Is she a vehicle for Jem, and the reader, as he vents his frustration at the attacks upon his father and his moral code? Do you regard Jem as 'brave' here – if so, is he defending his father or Tom Robinson? Does who he is defending alter your perception of his bravery – is it 'brave', in this novel, to fight for some causes and not for others?

— Look back over your answers to these questions as you work through your analysis. Do your responses change? Does the incident with Mrs Dubose become thematically relevant later in the novel? Consider how your attitude to other characters may have been influenced by this very deliberate discussion of 'bravery' before the focus of the novel becomes Tom Robinson's trial.

EXTEND . . .

— You may want to extend this analysis even further to consider how our attitudes to bravery have altered historically. This text was set before the Second World War and the Holocaust. Have major historical traumas changed our ideas about what it means to be brave?

PART TWO

CHAPTER 12
(pp. 127–39)

Focus on: difference

DISTINGUISH . . .

— This chapter focuses on Jem and Scout's trip to Calpurnia's church. Pick out the particular words and phrases that establish the differences between the two communities. How is the black community distinguished here from the white community? Are any particular distinctions made within the black community? How, for example, is Calpurnia differentiated from her fellow worshippers?

EVALUATE . . .

— Use your analysis of the text to evaluate the treatment of differences between the black and white communities within the novel. Which differences are highlighted? Are there any distinctions that blur the boundaries, for example, or are all the differences absolute?

— Take your analysis a step further and consider the placement of this focus on difference. Why does Part Two of the text open with this particular journey? What kind of relationship does it establish between the protagonists and the black community? Where does it place the reader: what kind of relationship does it establish between the reader and the black characters in the novel?

CHAPTER 13
(pp. 140–8)

Focus on: family

CONSTRUCT AND INTERROGATE . . .

Aunt Alexandra moves to Maycomb and establishes herself as part of the family network at the opening of this chapter.

> 'Have you come for a visit, Aunty?' I asked. [. . .]
> 'Well, your father and I decided it was time I came
> to stay with you for a while.'
> 'For a while' in Maycomb meant anything from three
> days to thirty years (p. 140).

— Taking evidence from this chapter, construct this family as you perceive it. How do you define familial relationships? Is 'blood' the defining factor for you? If not, what rules or codes construct a family? How do you know that you belong to a family? What customs does our culture set in place to regulate familial membership?

— When you have drawn up your version of this family, get together and compare your family groups. What differences do you note? For example, have you included physically absent members of the family, or is membership defined primarily by proximity?

DISCUSS . . .

— Employ the differences between your models as a starting point for a discussion on how families are constructed. Contemporary society contains complex negotiations of family units – think about adoption, fostering, second and third marriages, common-law marriages, same-sex marriages, or relationships that we take to be established but which are not sanctioned by the institution of marriage.

— The family unit in *To Kill a Mockingbird* is equally complicated. Do you regard the novel as being less fluid in its conception of family than contemporary culture? If not, why not? Draw evidence from the text as a whole: do not focus solely on this chapter, and remember to include characters such as Miss Rachel and Dill, Calpurnia, Tom Robinson and Boo.

CHAPTER 14
(pp. 148–59)

Focus on: authority

COMPARE AND CONTRAST . . .

— Scout challenges Aunt Alexandra's authority when she is forbidden to visit Calpurnia's house (p. 149). This is followed by Dill's arrival at the house having run away from his parents (pp. 153–9). Look at the treatment of authority in these episodes. How is authority characterised differently in terms of the two families?

— Use the different episodes to explore the versions of authority you are presented with here. Think particularly about the relationship of respect to authority. Do the children obey because of fear, or because the authority figure has earned their respect? You may want to bring in evidence from elsewhere in the novel.

CHARACTERISE . . .

— Atticus is a figure of authority throughout the novel. You could extend your analysis by drawing a character sketch of Atticus, focusing entirely on the idea of him as a figure of authority. How is he characterised in relation to his power within the community?

CHAPTER 15
(pp. 159–71)

Focus on: empathy

DEFINE AND EXAMINE . . .

— This chapter functions primarily as an exercise in empathy. Before starting your analysis, establish that you understand the term. What examples would you use to explain its subtleties to someone else? How is it different from sympathy, for example?

— When you are clear about the term, examine this chapter, thinking about it as an extended example of empathy. How is empathy characterised here? Would you describe it as an active or a passive response? Which characters demonstrate empathy for one another? How are some characters forced to empathise, despite their resistance?

— Also look at the treatment of empathy as a weapon. How is it used to disarm? How does Lee suggest that it is more powerful than physical force?

EXPLORE . . .

— You might want to use your examination of empathy in this chapter as a model for the text as a whole. Think about how it offers a model both for the characters within the novel and for the reader. How does the text influence you to empathise with the characters the text privileges as being worthy of empathy? Are any characters denied empathy? (You could come back to this question when you have completed your study of the whole novel.)

CHAPTER 16
(pp. 171–82)

Focus on: audiences

ESTABLISH . . .

— Before you turn your attention to the text, note down the kinds of occasions you expect to have an 'audience'. Develop your list as fully as you can: think about how much of contemporary entertainment is about 'watching', or being an audience to, unusual situations, such as the TV programme *Big Brother*.

ASSESS . . .

— When you have fully established the various kinds of audiences you are familiar with, assess how audiences have different expectations, and behave differently. For example, how does a football audience at a live match behave in comparison to a cinema audience or an audience at an opera?

REASSESS . . .

— Use your, now more sophisticated, analysis of audiences to critique the audience Jem and Scout witness on their way to the trial. What kind of expectations would you construct from what you are told about the audience? How does its makeup surprise you? Is there only one audience, or is the trial witnessed by multiple audiences? Unpack the different audiences you identify, and be clear about how their expectations are different or contradictory.

CHAPTER 17
(pp. 183–97)

Focus on: court dramas

PONDER . . .

— The court scene is an important one in American culture. You may want to compare and contrast this scene with the treatment of the trial in *Native Son*, or you may want to draw on other literary models. You could look at Nathaniel Hawthorne's *The Scarlet Letter* (1850) and its treatment of the trial and punishment of a criminal, or Herman Melville's 'Benito Cereno' (1856) which also deals with the idea of innocence and how the court deals with the guilty. You could even look at popular novelists such as John Grisham, a best-selling writer who constantly reworks the trial ethic in his novels.

— Focus your attention now upon the chapter that introduces the trial scene and think about why this trial is the central episode of the novel. What thematic concerns does it represent? The novel has a political and moral agenda – so what values does the trial represent? How is that agenda presented here?

— The idea of the trial as a bastion of democracy is central to one of the text's major concerns. You could extend this analysis by looking over the novel, focusing your attention on its treatment of democracy. How is it highlighted within the text? Which characters represent the democratic principle?

Focus on: white trash

REVISE . . .

— Look back to the exercise that focuses on 'class' on pp. 93–4 of this guide. If you did not complete the task at that point, work through the exercise as a whole now, conducting the research suggested there. If you have already

III

completed that section, then just refresh your memory about your research. What did you establish was 'white trash'? How does it fit in a black/white-class hierarchy?

CHARACTERISE . . .

— When you are clear about the term 'white trash', turn your attention to this chapter and look at the testimonies of Heck Tate and Bob Ewell. Would you characterise either of these men as 'white trash'? If so, why? (Be sure to support your responses with textual evidence.)

— Complete your character analysis and use the evidence you have produced to question *why* Lee paints a character as 'white trash'. How does it alter your perception of their evidence? Does it discredit them? If so, how?

QUESTION . . .

— Having analysed how the treatment of a character as 'white trash' changes your attitude to their credibility as accusers, think about the larger consequences of this for the novel.

— Use these questions as starting points:

• How is the status of the white community maintained when it is established that the man accusing Tom Robinson is 'white trash'?

• How is the black community represented here in relation to 'white trash' – are they equals? Is the black community superior? What are the consequences for the black community in your assessment?

CHAPTER 18
(pp. 197–209)

Focus on: desire

LIST . . .
— Look at Mayella's testimony and pick out the different kinds of desire characterised here. Use the list below as a starting point, but add your own versions of desire, developing your list as widely as possible. Include evidence from this chapter to support your inclusion of particular kinds of desire.

● Sexual – lust
● Communal – the desire for company
● Physical – the desire for proximity/warmth
● Emotional – the desire to be loved
● Social – the desire to be socially acceptable/respected, to be considered attractive
● Psychological – the desire to be treated as an individual/adult/equal

INTERPRET . . .
— When you have considered the varied nature of desire, interpret its complexity in this chapter. Is Tom the sole focus of desire in this chapter? Who else does Mayella desire? Who desires her – is that desire appropriate? Do some desires affect, or even contradict, one another?
— Think about how complex an emotion is represented here, even as one character is compromised by conflicting desires.

PERSONALISE . . .
— You could extend your discussion of Mayella's complex desires by thinking about situations when your desires have contradicted themselves. Think about how you handled that

difficulty. Did you always honour other people's desires over and above your own?

— Does personalising that question change your attitude to Mayella's behaviour? In what ways does recognising the complexity of desire make analysing others', even literary figures', behaviour more complex?

CHAPTER 19
(pp. 209–20)

Focus on: Tom Robinson

DETAIL . . .

— By looking closely at the information you are given about Tom Robinson through his testimony, construct a detailed character analysis of him. As part of your examination include Atticus's reaction to him – how does this influence your assessment of Tom's character?

— You are given important details about Tom's physical make-up: how does this alter your perception of him as a character? Does it confirm your position as to whether or not you perceive him to be an 'innocent man'? If so, what impact does this have on your character analysis?

COLLATE . . .

— Combine your individual characterisations. How easy is it to come up with a single version of Tom? Is his characterisation complex? If so, what complicates it?

— If, however, you do not find it difficult to construct Tom's character, think about *why* Lee creates such a clear, or simple, picture of Tom. What purpose does this characterisation serve in terms of the novel's plot and thematic concerns? Why is it important that Tom is not a questionable character?

Focus on: stereotypes

CONSIDER YOUR OWN IDEAS CAREFULLY . . .

— The idea that the ultimate object of desire for the black man is a white woman is a central myth in American culture. Novels such as James Fenimore Cooper's, *The Last of the Mohicans* (1826), Margaret Mitchell's *Gone With the Wind* (1936) or even, in fact, Puritan settlers' narratives, such as Anne Bradstreet's account of her arrival in America, deal with the prospect of the white woman's rape.

— Before tackling the text, it is important to clarify the term 'rape fantasy' as a stereotype. Use the glossary to give you a working definition and discuss the issue with others to get a larger perspective.

— Make sure that you are clear that 'fantasy' is not being used here in terms of *desire*. Rather, it is employed here as meaning an 'idea' or possibility. Have you come across this stereotype before (you might want to think about how it has changed in contemporary culture)?

— In order to fully explore the importance of 'rape' in twentieth-century American literature, see the Contexts section entitled 'Rape' for this novel (on pp. 134–6).

EMPLOY . . .

— The idea of the black man ravishing the white woman informs much of this novel. Throughout this section Atticus fights to establish Tom's innocence. Look closely at the language here and pick out examples that suggest Atticus's knowledge of the stereotypes being applied to Tom. How is his examination of Tom informed by what he knows of American myths about the black man?

EXTEND . . .

As you work your way through the novel come back to these

stereotypes and think about how they are employed. Which characters invoke them? Who repudiates them?

CHAPTER 20
(pp. 220–7)

Focus on: appearances versus reality

PARALLEL . . .

— Look at this apparent shift in narrative. The story leaves the courtroom and moves outside to a marginal character, Mr Raymond, and his conversation with Dill and Scout.

— Analyse this chapter, focusing upon how it parallels the themes privileged in the court scene. Be aware that the incident outside the courtroom works on more than one level: not only do the characters discuss the action, suggesting viewpoints not normally placed in the mouths of respectable characters, but the incident also acts as a parable for the trial.

CREATE . . .

— Identify the parable the children learn from Mr Raymond. Look back over your discussion of myths and fairy stories. These tales commonly include lessons for the reader, but it is disguised in the action here. How does this text disguise its parable?

— Create your own fairy story or parable in which you disguise the lesson you have taken from this chapter of *To Kill a Mockingbird*. Bear in mind that the story needs to entertain, or the reader will become aware that s/he is being 'taught' and cease reading your 'story'.

CHAPTER 21
(pp. 227–33)

Focus on: juries

DISCOVER . . .

— This chapter gives an account of the jury delivering its verdict. Conduct some research into the jury system in America. Use the following questions as starting points:

- For how long have juries been a part of the justice system of the United States?
- How many people make up a jury?
- When were women first allowed to sit on juries?
- What qualifies a person for jury service? Can anyone sit on a jury? What limits apply – age/colour/criminal record/professional/health?
- Are jury members vetted – if so, by whom?
- Who can ask for a member of the jury to be dismissed and replaced?
- What are the acceptable grounds for dismissing a jury member?

CONSIDER . . .

— When you have completed your research, take some time to consider how your increased understanding of the system affects your attitude to the idea of the jury.

— Think about how complex a jury system is. What values, for example, does Scout perceive complicate the jury in this text? (Take textual evidence from beyond the chapter.)

EXTEND . . .

— You may want to take some time to discuss the jury system. Do you regard it as a fundamentally positive form of justice?

Has your attitude to juries changed as a result of your focus on it here? Remember to bear in mind that the American jury system has important differences from the British one. You may want to talk through a particular American case, such as the prosecution of the policemen accused of assaulting and killing Rodney King. How does racism complicate the idea of the jury? Another useful resource here may be the film *Twelve Angry Men* (1957) directed by Sidney Lumet.

CHAPTER 22
(pp. 234–9)

Focus on: change

DETAIL AND EXPLORE . . .

— Take this short chapter and explore the theme of change. How does the narrative (pick out particular words and phrases) suggest a shift from the optimism of the opening of the novel? Look particularly at the character of Jem – how is the treatment of his adolescence used to suggest maturing attitudes within the novel? You may want to explore the idea of growing up beyond this particular chapter. Keep your attention focused on Jem, but look at the idea of his becoming a man, and how it parallels the increasing complexity of the world encountered throughout the novel.

CHAPTER 23
(pp. 239–51)

Focus on: hierarchies

DELINEATE . . .

— Tease out the different and complex hierarchies explored within this chapter. Seeing these hierarchies literally will clarify the power relationships you have identified.

— Draw yourself a staircase (you may want to do this individually or as a group) and write out the names of the characters both directly referred to here, and those whose presence is implied. Place the characters on your staircase, demonstrating the power structure as you perceive it. Tom Robinson may be at the base of your staircase, but is Bob Ewell lower? Where do children fit in this hierarchy – and does gender affect their status? Are Dill and Scout on the same step? Discuss your reasons for placing characters in their relative positions.

DEVELOP . . .

— As you work your way through this spatial version of these power structures, the complexity of these relationships is highlighted. One of the problems you will have encountered in this exercise is that these relationships are not static, rather they shift as people try to maintain authority over one another. This is shown in Scout's conversation with Aunt Alexandra as Scout struggles to promote Walter Cunningham and Aunty resists (p. 247).

— Develop the exercise by focusing on the text's treatment of hierarchy. For example, in this struggle is Scout supported by Atticus, or does he uphold Alexandra's position? Think about whether hierarchies are subverted or sustained here – are some upheld while others are made problematic? You may want to come back to these issues when you have completed your analysis. Does your attitude change when you consider the novel as a whole?

CHAPTER 24
(pp. 251–62)

Focus on: femininity

ANALYSE . . .

— 'They had spent two afternoons at the creek, they said they were going in naked and I couldn't come' (p. 251). 'I was wearing my pink Sunday dress, shoes, and a petticoat, and reflected that if I spilled anything Calpurnia would have to wash my dress again for tomorrow' (pp. 252). In this episode both Scout and the reader are properly introduced to the feminine world of Maycomb for the first time. Work your way through the chapter, focusing particularly upon the treatment of femininity here. How is the 'feminine' characterised? You could start your analysis by looking at the treatment of 'ladylike' appearance, as highlighted above. Then extend your analysis to include other facets of 'femininity' – how do 'ladies' speak, act, behave? What are the codes they are supposed to adhere to according to this chapter? Look particularly at Miss Maudie's defence of the Finches (p. 256–7), or Alexandra's behaviour after she hears of the death of Tom Robinson (pp. 259–62). How do these sub-narratives indicate a feminine code? How do they demonstrate how women are supposed to behave?

EVALUATE . . .

— When you have completed your analysis of 'femininity' in this chapter, broaden your focus and interrogate the idea of 'femininity' itself. Look up 'feminine' in a dictionary – how is it

defined? Does this definition fit with your analysis of the text?
— Consider also the extent to which you regard 'femininity' as a contemporary construct. We still understand the phrase 'ladylike', which would suggest that it is still a meaningful construct. How would you define 'femininity', and how radically does your definition differ from the version you have gleaned from the novel?

CHAPTER 25
(pp. 262–6)

Focus on: narrative style/narrative devices

INTERROGATE . . .
— 'According to Dill, he and Jem had just come to the highway when they saw Atticus driving towards them' (p. 264). Think about the employment of plot devices here. The author has decided that she wants the reader to witness Atticus's encounter with Tom's wife. Concentrate your analysis on how the text is constructed in order to allow this to happen plausibly for the reader. How does the text ensure that we will not be surprised by Jem's 'chance encounter' with his father? Look back to the previous chapter and think about how the novel establishes this plot device. Why is this device necessary? Would it be appropriate for Atticus simply to narrate this visit on his return home from work – why might the reader reject this?

CHOOSE . . .
— When you have looked closely at this plot device, find another example from somewhere else in the text. How do you characterise this example? How does it move the plot of the novel forward? Does it provide an opportunity to give the reader vital information?

PONDER . . .

— Think about how these plot devices are disguised, or naturalised, so that the reader's attention is not drawn to the device itself, but accepts it as part of the novel. How was the example you chose cloaked to make it a seamless part of the action? Were you prepared for it by previous textual references – how was it set up?

CHAPTER 26
(pp. 266–73)

Focus on: history

ASSESS . . .

— 'We are a democracy' (p. 270). Look at the treatment of 'history' in this chapter. What year was this novel published? Find out a little about the time at which this novel came out, and think about how that very different history may affect readings of the novel. For example, the text refers to 'Hitler' (p. 271). Had the Second World War taken place when this novel was set, or when it was published? Was the Holocaust a public fact? Think about how historical context changes our reading. Would we read with the same attitude if we didn't know the outcome of the war?

— Think about how historical knowledge affects our readings. What major historical factors do you, as a group, regard as particularly important in framing your analysis of this text? (You may want to use the Contexts section on pp. 131–37 to expand this analysis.)

CHAPTER 27
(pp. 273–80)

Focus on: superstition

RECALL . . .

— Before focusing your attention on the text, try and identify superstitions that you have believed in. Work as a group and compare and contrast your recollections. Is there any pattern to the superstitions that you found convincing? What links can you draw between them? Is there any difference between genders in the superstitions that you have noted? Do any of them operate by implying changes to the body itself? Are superstitions threatening? If so, in what ways?

RELATE . . .

— Use your recollections of superstition to discuss the two episodes that dominate this chapter, Bob Ewell's attacks (pp. 273–76) and the terrorising of Misses Tutti and Frutti (pp. 277–8). What differentiates one episode from the other? Which of these would you categorise as a 'superstition'?

— Think about how superstition is undermined in both tales. How is Ewell's behaviour established as a continuing threat? Concentrate on the relationship of this to superstition – do we consider superstitions to be harmless fun, and thus characterised by Misses Tutti and Frutti, or are they a way of controlling malign forces through language?

REFLECT . . .

— You may want to extend your analysis to incorporate the text as a whole and reflect upon the novel's treatment of Boo. What superstitions operate in relation to him? Do Jem and Scout engineer these superstitions, or are they informed by other characters' attitudes to the family?

123

— Take some time to consider the employment of superstition in this narrative. How is it used to signal certain plot twists and characterisations in this novel? You could contrast the treatment of Boo with that of Bob Ewell – what kind of superstitious narratives encapsulate them?

CHAPTER 28
(pp. 280–94)

Focus on: comedy

DESCRIBE . . .

— Look closely at the employment of comedy in this chapter. Pick out the events, characters, words and phrases that are included to provide comic relief. Describe, for example, the party and the fancy-dress costumes – how are they 'comic'?

COMPARE AND CONTRAST . . .

— Take a tragedy you are familiar with, such as *Othello, Hamlet* or *Macbeth*, and look at Shakespeare's use of comedy. Can you identify comic scenes – what purpose do they serve? Do they provide light relief from the action? Do they parallel the tragedy's concerns, but by presenting them in a different fashion, highlight different aspects?

— Use your consideration of a tragedy to compare and contrast the treatment of comedy in *To Kill a Mockingbird*. Is comedy used in a similar fashion? How does it alter pace? Does it parallel the more serious concerns of the novel? How is this lighter scene used to introduce important plot details?

— Do you notice marked differences in the treatment of comedy in your example and this text? Or is it employed in a similar fashion? Think about comedy as a literary tool. Are you surprised to identify comic scenes in the most tragic of texts?

How important is it to vary tone and style, from the comic to the tragic? Would you want to define this text as a tragedy, a tragicomedy, a comedy, or would you use another term?

CHAPTERS 29 AND 30
(pp. 294–305)

Focus on: inside versus outside

EXAMINE . . .
— As Ewell's death is discussed, examine the treatment of 'outsiders' over the course of these two chapters. How are Ewell and Boo set up in opposition to one another, one as a physical outsider, but morally and socially included, the other as a social outsider whose physical presence has been clearly felt by the community as a whole?

REVISE . . .
— You may want to look over your discussion of 'white trash' at this point (the focus of discussion for Chapters 3 and 17). How does it inform the treatment of inside versus outside here? Is Boo also excluded on grounds of class, or does his family's status secure him a place in the Maycomb community?

DISTINGUISH . . .
— Using your analysis of white trash, and how it places Ewell as an outsider in this community, pick out the other phrases that identify Ewell as an outsider. How, for example, does his behaviour isolate him? How does the treatment of his death by the community further distinguish him as not belonging?

Focus on: justice

DISCUSS . . .

— Work in small groups (fours or fives) and discuss the treatment of justice in these two chapters. How do you react to this treatment of his death? Do you agree with the Maycomb sheriff, or are you more in agreement with Atticus who is reluctant but agrees in the end, or do you dismiss the treatment entirely and regard it as a miscarriage of justice? Is Bob Ewell the novel's victim, or is his death justifiable revenge for Tom Robinson's death?

COMBINE . . .

— Take the notes you have made in this discussion and combine them with your analysis of the insider versus outsider.

— In combining your analyses, think about how the novel successfully disposes of its three 'outsiders'; the community's equilibrium is restored as Boo is fully integrated, however reluctantly, into the community by his action; and Ewell and Robinson are removed. Is this a problem, as the white middle class is restored as unquestionably in charge? How does this alter your attitude to Robinson's death?

— Consider carefully the novel's resolution here – what sort of questions does it raise for you about the novel's treatment of race and hierarchy?

CHAPTER 31
(pp. 305–9)

Focus on: endings

ANALYSE AND INTERPRET . . .

— Question the novel's ending. You are provided with the

text's resolution in the previous two chapters, as Ewell's death is confirmed and his murderer protected, so how would you interpret the function of this final chapter?

— Look particularly at the passage of time traced here – how is it markedly different from the preceding two chapters? Why does the novel narrate the passage of the novel in just two pages (pp. 307–8)? How is the narrator different for this segment of text? Why does it return to the 'present' with Atticus's vigilance over Jem?

PARALLEL . . .

— If you tackled the exercise where you focused on comedy on pp. 124–5 look back over the end of the play that you selected. If, however, that is not an exercise you have attempted, choose a Shakespeare tragedy, preferably one you are in some way familiar with, and examine the structure of the ending, paralleling it with this novel. How is catharsis constructed by continuing the action beyond the resolution of the text? Is the action of the play recapped in the closing scene of the tragedy you have chosen? If so, what narrative function might this have?

REASSESS AND ANALYSE . . .

— When you have thought about the structure of endings, turn your attention back to *To Kill a Mockingbird*. How does the closing chapter focus the text thematically? If you were to tease out the novel's concerns from the final chapter alone, what themes do you consider are highlighted? Do they reflect your analysis of the text as a whole?

Looking over the whole novel

QUESTIONS FOR DISCUSSION OR ESSAYS

1. Would you characterise *To Kill a Mockingbird* as a Christian novel?

2. In what ways does the distinction between the 'white' community and the 'white trash' community create a false distinction?

3. Think about the treatment of Tom Robinson and Mayella in the novel as a whole. How is he used to complicate the binary opposition of 'guilty versus innocent'?

4. To what extent does the history of the 'South', or more particularly Alabama, inform this novel? Do you have to understand the novel's historical context in order to enjoy the story? To what extent does the novel cut across the place and time of its setting?

5. 'In order to understand the text fully it is crucial to know the biography of Lee, and particularly her childhood.' Discuss.

6. *To Kill a Mockingbird* offers a particular version of femininity throughout the novel. How would you define the model the text offers you?

7. Is the idea of empathy a central literary construct at work in this novel? What other literary devices have you become aware of in your reading – how do they influence your interpretation of the novel?

8. 'Black masculinity and the idea of the black man as rapist is successfully debunked in this novel.' Discuss.

9. 'I wanted you to see what real courage is, instead of getting the idea that courage is a man with a gun in his hand' (p. 124). Who do you regard as the most courageous character in this novel, and how is their 'courage' characterised?

10. In what ways do the childrens' games and dramas relate to the games and dramas played out by the adults in the novel?

11. Discuss the theme of boundaries in the novel.

12. Discuss the use of symbols and symbolism in the novel.

13. Examine the ways in which the characters' language reflects their attitudes and prejudices in the novel.

14. Harper Lee has called her novel 'a love story'. To what extent do you agree with this characterisation of the novel.

Contexts, comparisons and complementary readings

These sections suggest contextual and comparative ways of reading the four novels in this volume. Here, the focus is Harper Lee and *To Kill a Mockingbird*. You can put your reading in a social, historical or literary context. You can make comparisons – again, social, literary or historical – with other texts or art works. Or you can choose complementary works (of whatever kind) – that is, art works, literary works, social reportage or facts which in some way illuminate the text, by giving a framework to references you currently find oblique. Some of the suggested contexts are directly connected to the book, in that they will give you precise literary or social frames in which to situate the novel. In turn, these are either related to the period within which the novel is set, or to the time – now – when you are reading it. Some of these examples are designed to suggest books or other texts that may make useful sources for comparison (or for complementary purposes) when you are reading *To Kill a Mockingbird*. Again, they may be related to literary or critical themes, or they may be relevant to social and cultural themes current 'then' or 'now'.

The first two contexts for Lee raise identical concerns to those tackled in relation to Wright. This is important, as the novels share not only their historical context (although they were published twenty years apart), but also their thematic concerns – the possibility of rape, and its relationship to representations of black masculinity, means that these contexts are relevant to both.

Focus on: the history and legacy of slavery

RESEARCH . . .

— *To Kill a Mockingbird* is predicated upon the history of slavery and an understanding of the American South. The London folio edition includes an introduction by Albert French, in which he emphasises the importance of Lee's treatment of racial stereotyping and the ostracising of the black American community. The position of the black community in relation to the white residents of Maycomb is the anxious centre of the novel. Think, for example, about Jem and Scout's trip to church with Calpurnia – the link between the continued oppression of the black community, and its relationship to the history of that community, is clearly established.

Using the bibliography, as well as the Internet and libraries to which you have access, create a working knowledge of the historical context of the novel. You will find the 'American Memory' website at the Library of Congress useful. Below is a list of key terms – use them as a means of starting your investigation by discovering what these terms mean.

- Negro
- Emancipation
- Abolitionists
- Civil War
- Segregation

— When you are clear about these specific terms, extend your research. Think about what it means to demarcate identities along colour lines. Through your research you will also have come across some discussion of the consequences of segregation – what it means to be allowed to sit only in one part of a bus, or to be forced to use a different toilet to the white community. This will be developed later, but bear in mind the value judgements being instituted here.

— Next, look into the following phrases, the historical keynotes that mark our understanding of the slave trade, and the history of segregation it has established. What specific identifications, events and practices do they refer to?

- Institution of slavery
- One-Drop Rule
- Dixie
- Jim Crow
- Nigger
- White trash

— Find out when segregation was formally ended in the United States – does how recent the date is shock you?

COMPARE . . .

— Compare Lee's novel with Harriet Beecher Stowe's *Uncle Tom's Cabin*. Stowe's novel is said to have inspired Lincoln to support emancipation, which led to the American Civil War. Look at Stowe's treatment of black identity. This comparison is particularly important because both novels foreground Christianity. Would you describe both as 'Christian' novels? How do Christian themes link the texts? Do they both present a 'right' and a 'wrong' version of how white Christians behave?

— You may want to compare Lee's treatment of the history of the black community with Richard Wright's novel. Both texts focus on the same period – are they informed by a similar understanding of the history and legacy of slavery? How does your research temper your response to *To Kill a Mockingbird*?

Focus on: rape

WE RECOGNISE . . .
This *Vintage Living Text* acknowledges the brutal reality of rape statistics in the United Kingdom.

- 1 in 4 women suffer rape or attempted rape
- The most common rapists are current and ex-husbands or current and ex-partners
- 1 in 7 married women say they have been forced to have sex, compared to 1 in 3 divorced or separated women
- 91 per cent of women tell no one

Source: Kate Painter (1991)
www.rapecrisis.co.uk/statistics.htm 17/10/02

ESTABLISH . . .
— Notice that in the context of *To Kill a Mockingbird*, rape is employed as a political and cultural act and motif. This is clearly demonstrated in Lee's novel, as the rape *does not take place*. Tom Robinson undermines the racist stereotype of the powerful black man not only because the act did not occur, but also because Lee deliberately removes Tom's power from him by giving him a withered arm. Not only does he not rape Mayella; he is not actually physically capable of doing so.

DISCOVER . . .
— The idea of rape is important in both a literary and a historical context. Look over the list below and bear in mind its historical scope.

- The Greek legend of *Tereus and Philomela*
- *The Rape of Lucrece* (William Shakespeare)
- *Titus Andronicus* (William Shakespeare)
- *The Rape of the Lock* (Alexander Pope)
- *Charlotte Temple* (Susanna Rowson)
- 'Leda and the Swan' (W. B. Yeats)
- *Gone with the Wind* (Margaret Mitchell)
- 'Act of Union' (Seamus Heaney)

— This list is deliberately disparate – it covers many centuries, includes writers from more than one country, and features plays, poems and novels. You may want to read one of the titles – some are parodies, some do not even refer to human individuals, but they employ rape, instead, in the context of one nation's relationship with another or as a metaphor for other kinds of assault.

— The particular importance of your discovery of these texts is that 'rape' here is not necessarily a literal act. Often the rape itself does not take place, but the fear of it dominates the text. Look closely at its treatment as a *metaphor* here, and establish what rape means as a metaphor. What sort of power relationship does it represent?

HISTORICISE . . .

— When you have established 'rape' as a metaphor, its particular context in American culture is your next focus. The 'fantasy' or 'fear' of black masculinity has been a central cultural concern, which was established during America's period of slavery, and reinforced after the Civil War. In order to appreciate this history, look at Toni Morrison's *Playing in the Dark: Whiteness and the Literary Imagination* (1992), and her collection of essays *Race-ing Justice, En-gendering Power: Essays on Anita Hill, Clarence Thomas, and the Construction of Social Reality* (1993).

135

— Through your historicisation you are forming an under-standing of the centrality of 'rape fantasy' to American cul-ture. You have examined it in its literary form and come to know something of its historical background. To what extent has this deepened understanding altered your attitude to *To Kill a Mockingbird*?

Focus on: the Scottsboro boys' trial

RESEARCH . . .

Perhaps one of the most famous trials in American history, and certainly one of the most contentious, was the trial of the Scottsboro boys. It involved the alleged gang rape of two white girls by nine black teenagers on the Southern Railroad freight, run from Chattanooga to Memphis, on 25 March 1931.

— Using the Internet, find out as much as you can about this particular case. Why has its history been so contentious? Was it considered to be particularly important in relation to the Southern states of America?

LINK . . .

— When you have researched this trial, link your material to Lee's novel. How does this particular case inform the debates Lee considers? Bear in mind that although the novel is set in the 1930s it was written in the late 1950s. What kind of com-mentary, if any, is Lee making about this particular case? Or do you consider the novel to link to the trial more broadly – what issues does Lee raise that connect *To Kill A Mockingbird* to the Scottsboro boys?

TALK THROUGH . . .

— Discuss the connections between the historical incident and the novel's thematic concerns. How does it change your attitude to the text? Does it make you regard it as a more 'accurate' novel? Are you encouraged to read biographically? You might want to follow up other connections with Lee and her history. The character of Dill, for example, is possibly based on the author Truman Capote, who lived next door to Lee. Find out about Capote. Does your knowledge of him change your idea of the characterisation of Dill? Does the intrusion of biographical and historical reading complicate your reading? If so, how? Think over how these 'facts' change your attitude to the text.

Focus on: Emmett Till

RESEARCH . . .
— Another famous case was that of Emmett Till a fourteen-year-old black boy who was murdered in Mississippi in 1955. Research the event and why it was the focus of so much contention at the time. Link this material to the debates that Lee considers.

Focus on: Film adaptation

COMPARE . . .
In 1962 Robert Mulligan directed Gregory Peck in a film adaptation of *To Kill A Mockingbird*. Watch the film and compare it with the novel. In particular, identify what has been changed or left out, and consider how successful the adaptation is.

The Catcher in the Rye

IN CLOSE-UP

Reading activities: detailed analysis

CHAPTER I
(pp. 1-5)

Focus on: storytelling

DETAIL . . .

— 'If you really want to hear about it, the first thing you'll probably want to know is where I was born, and what my lousy childhood was like, and how my parents were occupied and all before they had me, and all that David Copperfield kind of crap, but I don't feel like going into it, if you want to know the truth' (p. 1). Look closely at this opening and pick out the words and phrases that mark it as an opening to a story. How does it differ from traditional models for opening narratives, such as 'Once upon a time'? Think about what you expect from the opening of a novel – does this fit with your expectations? Be specific about the words and phrases that surprise you.

— This is a very deliberate opening – how does it mark itself out as a 'story'? Look, for example, at the literary reference within it. You could compare and contrast this opening with the opening of Charles Dickens's *David Copperfield* (1849–50) – what do you notice about this comparison? Why do you think Salinger deliberately invites it?

QUESTION . . .

— When you have looked closely at the construction of this opening, think about how it establishes expectations for the text as a whole. Use the following questions to stimulate your analysis:

- Who is the narrator of this novel – what do you know about him at this point in the novel?
- Who is he talking to – the 'you' mentioned in the opening sentence? Is 'you' singular, or plural?
- How would you characterise the tone of the story at its outset? Pick out words and phrases that support your characterisation – if you believe the tone is humorous, give an example.
- What tense is the novel written in? Look carefully at the opening chapter – you are told the novel's outcome on the opening page. How does making the novel retrospective alter your expectations?
- What do you expect from the novel at this point?

— Come back to your answers as you work your way through the novel. How do your responses alter? Revise your answers when your analysis is complete, but remember to trace the development of your thoughts. Your initial responses are *not wrong* – the differences in your ideas at different stages are very instructive as they demonstrate the pattern of your close reading, and the development of your ideas.

CHAPTER 2
(pp. 6–13)

Focus on: age versus youth

EXAMINE . . .

— In this chapter Holden visits Mr Spencer. Examine the treatment of age in this encounter. Does Holden respect Mr Spencer? Does he understand the wisdom the teacher tries to impart through their review of his essay (pp. 9–12)? Examine the treatment of disease. How does the text suggest a particular relationship between disease and the elderly – can you identify the particular sentences that suggest physical decay?

INVESTIGATE . . .

— When you have examined the treatment of ageing you are presented with, think about other versions of youthful perceptions of sickness and decay. Is the callousness of Holden's reaction to Spencer a common version of youth's reaction to the ageing body? Think both about your own experiences and about literary models for this opposition. You could compare Holden's reaction to Pip's in Charles Dickens's *Great Expectations* (1861) chapter 1 or chapter 8, for example. Or look at the treatment of physical decay in the Divine poems of the metaphysical poet John Donne – how does his account of physical decay radically differ from Holden's perception of Spencer?

DISCUSS . . .

— In small groups discuss this version of the elderly – if you perceived Holden to be disrespectful of age, is this something you identified in the other examples, whether personal or literary, that you considered? What differences did you note? Is there any fear in Holden's account?

— Talk through the idea that this is a 'modern', or contemporary, representation of a youthful perception of the elderly. Are we less respectful of older generations, and is this reflected in the novel?

CHAPTER 3
(pp. 14–22)

Focus on: truth

PICK OUT . . .
— 'I'm the most terrific liar you ever saw in your life' (p. 14). Select the different versions of 'lies' you are given in this chapter. Include those Holden narrates, as well as those forming the plot in this chapter. Who else, according to Holden, is not telling the truth, or not behaving honestly, in this chapter? How is their deceit characterised? What words does he use to characterise them?

DETERMINE . . .
— When you have selected your textual evidence use it to determine how the 'truth' is characterised here. What does Holden regard as 'lying'? How does he identify other people's subterfuges? Try and tease out the versions of the truth and lies this text presents you with.

COMPLICATE . . .
— This chapter is punctuated by references to narratives. When you have considered the text's version of the truth, think about how the idea of a story complicates the notion of 'truth' as invoked here. What role does truth play in storytelling – do we demand absolute truth from a text? In what ways do we expect stories to remain constant – what are the internal truths

a text must maintain in order for us to recognise it as a story, as opposed to a lie?

INTERROGATE . . .
— Take some time to consider these difficulties. The role of truth in literature is complex. Do we expect the narrator to be honest? At this early stage in the novel, does Holden's claim that he is a 'liar' mean that you perceive him to be an unreliable narrator?

CHAPTER 4
(pp. 23–30)

Focus on: jealousy

TEASE OUT . . .
— Consider the text's treatment of jealousy in Stradlater's relationship with Holden. Start by assessing the different forms of jealousy that operate in their friendship. Use the list below to start your analysis, and cite evidence to support your choices. You will also want to introduce your own terms, or redefine the ones you are offered to better suit your analysis.

- Physical
- Social
- Sexual
- Intellectual

ASSESS . . .
— Consider the extent to which jealousy informs Holden's attitude to Stradlater. How is Holden's jealousy conveyed to you, the reader – what narrative devices are employed in order to indicate it? For example, how does the text establish irony

so that the reader recognises it in Holden's description of him as 'handsome' and 'charming' (p. 29)?

— Think about how jealousy destabilises your attitude to the narrator at this point in the novel. How do you read differently when you are aware of emotions and their influence on the speaker? How does your perception of Holden's jealousy alter your attitude to Stradlater, for example?

CHAPTERS 5 AND 6
(pp. 31–40)

Focus on: the reader

IDENTIFY . . .

— 'I'm a pacifist, if you want to know the truth' (p. 40). Look over these two chapters, paying particular attention to the way the reader is addressed, and the information you are given about the text's protagonist and narrator. What are you told about Allie (p. 33) here and how does it affect your relationship to the narrator? Think also about how your reading is affected by being directly addressed by the narrator. Who do you identify Holden as speaking directly to? Is this a very deliberate narrative that consciously includes the reader, or is the audience specifically someone else?

ANALYSE YOUR OWN RESPONSES . . .

— When you have worked closely through these chapters thinking about how you, the reader, are involved in the narrative, think about why Salinger employs this narrative style. How is your reading affected by being directly addressed? In the Contexts section for this novel one of the discussions focuses upon psychoanalysis, and the idea that Holden is speaking to a therapist (pp. 176–8). How does this interpretation, the idea of Holden's story as therapy, change the position of the reader – if you are placed in the same position as the therapist, how does it alter your responses to what you are hearing?

— You may want to talk through your assessment. How have you responded differently by being directly addressed? How does the idea of the narrative as being 'therapeutic' influence your reading?

Focus on: aggression

LIST . . .

— Select the words you would consider to be swearing used in these two chapters. As you make your selections, keep a tally of the frequency with which they are used, so that you build up an overall perception of the way swear-words are employed here.

ESTABLISH . . .

— When you have built up a profile of the way swear words are used, find out the extent to which they have been considered shocking at the time the novel was published (1951). You might want to look at a newspaper, magazine or even a novel from 1951 and contrast the language used to that of these chapters.

— When you have established how offensive, and by implication aggressive, the language used in these chapters is, focus on the treatment of physical aggression. Who incites the fight between Stradlater and Holden (pp. 37–8)? What crucial role does inappropriate language play in this fight?

CONSIDER . . .

— We are used to thinking of aggression in physical terms; consider the notion that language can be employed as aggressively as fists in this section of the text. Think about how Holden is violent verbally; for example, in his account of Stradlater's encounter with Jane. You may want to extend your analysis of swearing, or inappropriate language, to incorporate the novel as a whole. How does Holden Caulfield employ aggressive language, what does it suggest about him as a character?

CHAPTERS 7 AND 8
(pp. 41–52)

Focus on: adolescence

DELINEATE . . .

— Use these two chapters to sketch out the text's versions of adolescence. What experiences, events and attitudes do you associate with adolescence – for example, look at the references to smoking (p. 42) and sex (p. 43). However, also consider how relationships with the adult world, characterised predominantly in relationships with parents (their own or other people's), occupies much of Chapter 8 (pp. 47–52). Pay particular attention to the conversation with Ernest's mother, and draw on it to develop your sketch of Holden as an adolescent.

— Use your analysis of the text to construct a definition of the adolescent – how would you define adolescence on the basis of this analysis? Remember to consider the importance of rebellion to your definition – to what extent does a teenager define him/herself against society and social rules as opposed to identifying with them?

PERSONALISE . . .

— Focus on your experience of adolescence – you could think about your own adolescence, or your children's, or you may prefer to focus on someone else you know. Be specific about the instances you recall that you would characterise as 'adolescent', and think about the extent to which your recollections fit with the definition you have constructed through your analysis. To what extent does the model you have constructed through the text work with the personal examples you have considered?

EXTEND . . .
— When you have tested out your model in relation to personal experience, you may want to broaden your analysis further to incorporate the novel as a whole. The Contexts section for this novel highlights its reception as the first text to chronicle the condition of the teenager (pp. 175–6) – a relatively new social invention. In order to really investigate this notion, you could extend your analysis of *The Catcher in the Rye* by continuing to sketch out your profile of adolescence as you read on.
— Also extend your analysis by considering how current you regard this model to be. Do the forms of rebellion, fundamental in a definition of adolescence, still carry the same force, or would you regard this version of the teenager to be a dated one?

CHAPTER 9
(pp. 53–9)

Focus on: New York

MAP . . .
— This chapter refers specifically to the city of New York. Obtain a map of the city and, as a group or class, trace the journey Holden makes and the places he refers to. Try to establish, through his references, a sense of the city's make-up. For example, does Holden stay in fashionable New York, or is he in the suburbs of the city?

INVESTIGATE . . .

— When you have spent some time looking at your map, and got some sense of its layout, use the following questions to develop your consideration:

- What is the ethnic make-up of the New York Holden inhabits?
- How does Holden travel around the city – by car/cab/ train/bus/on foot? What does this indicate to you about his social status as well as his version of New York?

COMPARE . . .

— You may want to compare this view of New York to Bigger's in *Native Son*. Do you regard these places as the same city? Where is the black community in Holden's New York? What does their absence signify? Think about the total absence as a form of oppression of unrepresented communities in the novel.

Focus on: voyeurism

ESTABLISH . . .

— Using the bibliography provided and perhaps in discussion with others, establish what you understand 'voyeurism' to mean. Talk through the term – do you regard it positively? What is its relationship to titillation – do you regard it as harmless or possibly even comic? Or is it rather an abuse, taking advantage of an innocent victim?

EXPLORE . . .

— When you have set up a working definition of voyeurism, look closely at Holden's observation of a gentleman in a hotel room (pp. 54–6). Examine this episode in the light of your definition. Would you consider Holden to be a voyeur at this point? Make sure you clarify your definition: what is it about the incident that characterises, or fails to characterise, him in that role? Is the subject being watched of any consideration when making your assessment?

— When you have assessed this passage, extend your analysis to consider the relationship of the reader to the voyeur. (If you completed the section on pp. 146–7 of this text that focused on the reader, look over your notes. If you did not, you may want to go back at this point and attempt the exercise.)

— In your earlier analysis you may have established the relationship of the reader to the therapist. An alternative reading is presented here: the reader could be understood as a voyeur peeping in on Holden's life, either by 'overhearing' his conversation with his therapist, or by watching the story as it plays out. Does this complicate your understanding of reading? Talk through this interpretation – do you regard the reader as a voyeur? What impact does this idea have on your interpretation of the role of the reader? Is your attitude influenced by the narrative style – what difference does the style in which the reader is addressed make to your interpretation?

CHAPTER 10
(pp. 60–8)

Focus on: alcohol

CONSTRUCT . . .
— Work your way through this chapter and construct an analysis of the different treatments alcohol receives. Think about its different purposes and use the list below as a starting point to express Holden's relationship to drink. Does Holden drink:

- to relax?
- for an anaesthetic?
- to give him courage?
- to make him an adult (both in other people's eyes and in his own)?
- because he is an alcoholic?
- to seduce (by providing others with alcohol)?
- to demonstrate his status (he is rich enough to buy expensive, sophisticated drinks)?
- to get drunk (and avoid being conscious and thus responsible)?

— You may want to develop this list, either by adding more reasons, or by qualifying some of the suggestions made here, but remember to support your argument with evidence from this chapter. Bear in mind that the opening of the chapter, before he is actually drinking, is important as it provides some of his motivation for going to the bar.

CONSIDER . . .
— When you have examined this chapter closely, take some time to consider the treatment of alcohol here. Has your analysis made alcohol a more complex subject than you may have first imagined? If so, how has it altered your perception? You may want to broaden your analysis to look at the treatment of alcohol in the text as a whole. Getting drunk is not a simple activity in this text. Its motivation is complex, as are the feelings and responses it provokes in Holden here.
— When you have considered the complexity of alcohol here, think about how it parallels the novel thematically. Holden spends, for example, a great deal of time trying, physically, to escape – how is this paralleled in his relationship to alcohol?
— You may also want to think about the relationship between storytelling and drinking. Do you associate drunkenness with

being voluble? Do people remember the stories they have drunkenly told when they sober up? Equally, do you associate drunkenness with honesty? Do you regard drunkenness as a state where an individual is more likely to bare their soul? Draw upon literary and cultural role models for this, and think about filmic and television treatments of drunkenness, as well as your own experience where relevant. When you have explored this relationship, turn your attention back to the text and think about Holden's narrative as motivated by alcohol – is his 'tongue loosened', and does this possibility make his account less reliable? (Remember to be clear about the possible implications that you investigated in chapter 3.)

CHAPTER 11
(pp. 69–73)

Focus on: nostalgia

CHARACTERISE . . .

— This chapter focuses on Holden catching sight of Jane Gallagher. He gives a full account of their first encounter and subsequent friendship. Pick out the words and phrases that characterise Holden's account as 'nostalgic'. (If you are not sure of the term, use the glossary before you tackle the text.)

PARALLEL . . .

— In your characterisation, remember to bear in mind how your attitude to the narrator influences your reading. How are Holden's recollections of Jane different from his tone and style in other parts of the narrative? You may want to select his description of another character, for example Mr Spencer (pp. 6–8). How does his narration of events support a nostalgic reading of Chapter 11? Or you could look at his account of

Phoebe in the previous chapter (pp. 60–1) and note the similarities between his attitudes to these two characters.

CHAPTER 12
(pp. 74–9)

Focus on: phony

DEFINE . . .

— 'Lillian Simmons [. . .] Strictly a phony' (p. 78). Holden employs the term 'phony' throughout the text. Look at his conversation with Lillian and try to use it to establish what he means by phony here. What specific connotations does it have? Is it an insult? Through this particular encounter develop a working definition of phony as it is employed in this chapter.

FIND . . .

— When you have defined phony, look over the text and find other characters Holden identifies as 'phony'. Jot down a list and then work together as a group to construct as full a list as possible of the term's employment. (You may want to assign chapters to individuals to speed up the task.)

BROADEN . . .

— When you have constructed your list, use it to broaden your analysis of the term. (You may want to select a particular character from the list, or you might prefer to construct an argument taking the list as a whole.) Use the following questions to stimulate your analysis:

● How does the introduction of other characters undermine or sustain your definition?

- Are you surprised at the number of characters to whom the term is applied?
- What similarities do you spot between the characters you have listed – are they the same gender, age, class?
- Do you notice any particular characteristics of 'phoniness' that apply to the group as a whole?

CHAPTER 13
(pp. 80–8)

Focus on: value

COMPARE AND CONTRAST . . .

— 'Ya got a hanger? I don't want to get my dress all wrinkly. It's brand clean' (p. 86). In this chapter Holden hires a prostitute. Focus here on this encounter and compare and contrast the different values you are presented with. Begin with the most literal form of value: money. How do the characters respond differently to money? Does five dollars, for example, hold the same *value* for each of them? Does Holden spend money easily here? If not, why not, and how is his relationship to the value of money characterised differently to the prostitute's?

— When you have looked at value in monetary terms, think about the moral values you are presented with. Is the prostitute treated sympathetically, as an individual? Or is she a commodity, owned by Maurice and sold to Holden?

QUESTION . . .

— Use your analysis of value in this chapter to question the values the text establishes. How does Holden's access to money create a different set of values from the prostitute's or the pimp's? Question, for example, the code of value that establishes the prostitute as worthless, morally and economically, but fails to punish the person paying for the service to the same extent.

— Why is it that a prostitute can be guilty of soliciting but a client is not guilty of paying for sex? How would our perception of value alter if soliciting referred to people looking for sex in return for money?

— Think also about the value of money in terms of pricing sex. How do the two value systems – moral and economic – interlink? Think about the exchange of value: how easy is it to price a moral code that outlaws prostitution?

CHAPTERS 14 AND 15
(pp. 89–102)

Focus on: religion

DEFINE AND DESCRIBE . . .

— 'I felt like praying or something, when I was in bed, but I couldn't do it. I can't always pray when I feel like it. In the first place, I'm sort of an atheist' (p. 89). Look closely at these two chapters, focusing particularly on their discussion of religion. Pick out the religious references and consider their meanings. Make sure you understand the terms the novel employs. For example, what is an 'atheist'. What is a 'Catholic' (p. 101)? What is the difference between a Catholic and a Protestant (Holden's religion)?

— Look also at the treatment of religion through particular passages, or references to other texts. For example, explore the references to *Romeo and Juliet* (p. 100), or look at Holden's attempts at praying (pp. 89–90), or his observation of the nuns (p. 97).

— When you have examined these chapters' treatment of religion, try and describe the novel's attitude to religion here. Would you describe the text as 'Christian'? How would you describe the treatment of religion – is the novel ironic? Does it treat Christianity as a joke, or is the novel reverent in its attitude?

EVALUATE . . .

— As you attempt to describe the novel's attitude to religion, the complexity will be highlighted. For example, you may have described the novel's humorous treatment of religion, suggesting that it does not take religious subject matter too seriously. This, however, is complicated by the fact that Holden is attempting to pray.

— Take some time to work through these complexities – think particularly about how the novel's attitude could be described as contradictory. Look over your description of incidents and think about why Salinger includes a description of the nuns. What theme is established here?

— You may want to extend your analysis to look over the text as a whole. Does this contradictory attitude to religion inform the novel? Would you describe the novel as contradictory in its treatment of other themes? Is being contradictory part of being an adolescent?

CHAPTER 16
(pp. 103–10)

Focus on: childhood

ANALYSE . . .

— 'There was this record I wanted to get for Phoebe [. . .] It was about a little kid that wouldn't go out of the house because two of her front teeth were out and she was ashamed to' (pp. 103–4). Think about associations between certain places and interests. The zoo, for example, is a childlike location, unlike the opera. Now turn your attention to the text. How is childhood indicated here, through locations and styles for instance? Is the museum treated as a location for childhood? If so, how is this represented in the text?

ASSESS . . .

— When you have analysed the chapter's treatment of childhood locations, think about the idea of the museum itself. What do museums represent? How would you characterise them? What is their function? Who are they aimed at? How do they work?

— As part of your examination of museums, focus on the idea of the museum and its relationship to memory. Why is memory a particularly important concept here? As you work through these ideas, keep turning back to this chapter and look at Holden's memories of his visits to the museum (pp. 108–9). What do Holden's recollections suggest about the relationship between memory and museums? How do these ideas link back to a discussion of childhood?

TALK THROUGH . . .

— Get into groups and talk over your analysis of the museum in this chapter. Can you identify with Holden's attitude to the museum? Do you identify a particular location with the idea of childhood? Does Holden's memory highlight certain values of childhood, perhaps by suggesting that the museum is an important location in his childhood? In order to clarify this you may want to pick a particular childhood location. What values does it represent? (For example, if it were a beach holiday it might be freedom; or if it is a particular building, such as a visit to a fire station, perhaps it represented ambitions.)

— Clarify the values this representation of childhood highlights. Think about how Holden uses the museum to suggest differences between the values of childhood and his position now. (Bear in mind here that he feels unable to enter the museum.) What differences are highlighted, through the treatment of the museum, between adolescence and childhood?

CHAPTERS 17 AND 18
(pp. 111–27)

Focus on: escape

RESEARCH . . .

In this chapter Holden plans his escape from New York with Sally (p. 118). Travel and escape, whether fleeing poverty by moving west to new land, or east to the big city, are central themes in American literary history. The relationship between New York and the rest of America is also central. Holden mentions that some of the most famous twentieth-century American novels focus on escape: Ernest Hemingway's *A Farewell to Arms* (1929) and F. Scott Fitzgerald's *The Great Gatsby* (1925). Other seminal novels include John Steinbeck's *The Grapes of Wrath* (1939), and Jack Kerouac's *On the Road* (1957).

— Choose from these titles and research the idea of escape. You may want to choose one particular text and look at its treatment of travel between the East and West Coasts of America, or you could assign texts within a group in order to pool your research. Establish, through your analysis, an understanding of the importance of travel as a theme in twentieth-century American fiction.

CONSIDER . . .

— When you have researched the theme of travel across America, and its importance as a thematic concern, refocus your analysis on these chapters. How is travel treated here, as compared with the text you focused on in your research? Do you take Holden seriously – do you believe he is about to escape? If not, why not? How far does Holden actually travel in these chapters? How does he make his way around? What does this suggest about his ability to travel from state to state as he implies he will?

EXTEND . . .

— When you have discussed Holden's journeys in these chapters, extend your analysis to focus on the novel as a whole. Where is Holden as he narrates this novel? Is he in New York? Is he on the West Coast? What journeys does Holden narrate? Does the novel focus predominantly upon New York? Where does he travel to within the city?

— When you have examined the journeys Holden makes, contrast these with the journeys he *talks* about. In what ways does the narrative play with journeys? How do journeys that are not made, like the one in these chapters, influence the novel as a whole?

— Come back to these questions when you have completed your analysis. How has your attitude to the treatment of escape altered through your comparison with other texts, and in your examination of how journeys are employed in the novel?

Focus on: culture

LIST . . .

— In these two chapters Holden makes reference to a number of different plays, films and books. Pick out and list the particular cultural references made here. Include mentions of specific cultural locations and forms of music, as well as individual novels.

IDENTIFY . . .

— Work your way through your list, establishing what these cultural references mean. For example, what is 'Radio City' (p. 124)? What sort of paper is the *Saturday Evening Post* (p. 112)? Is it solely a New York publication, or is it printed across the States? Who is 'Emily Dickinson' (p. 126)? What nationality are the writers Holden mentions?

EXPLORE . . .

— When you have identified the specific meanings of the cultural references made in these chapters, think about what kind of tone they set. Why, for example, does the text deliberately refer to so many other American novelists? Does it, for example, suggest that this story (whether it's Holden's or Salinger's) regards itself as being in the same league? How do all these cultural references establish 'Americanness'? Do they reinforce your ideas about American culture? If so, how? If not, in what ways do they undermine your ideas about American culture?

LINK AND DISCUSS . . .

— Combine your analysis here with your examination of 'escape' in these two chapters. Would you characterise the novel's treatment of the theme of escape as 'American'? Has your research given you a more concrete idea of literary themes that are considered to be 'American'? How does your understanding of the references made to other American novels change your attitude to this novel? Has your analysis of the references to all forms of culture, from music and ice skating to Emily Dickinson, influenced your sense of what is distinctively American?

— Discuss your perception of American culture. Have these exercises changed your ideas about American culture – did you associate the United States with movies and not with novels, or were you already aware of its literary heritage?

— Talk through your different attitudes to 'Americanness', and turn your attention back to *The Catcher in the Rye*. Has your deepened understanding of American literary culture altered your reading of the novel?

CHAPTER 19
(pp. 128–34)

Focus on: the character of Luce

CHARACTERISE . . .
— This chapter highlights a number of the novel's thematic concerns. Before turning your attention to the themes specifically, focus on the character of Luce and produce a character analysis of him. Start with the physical description – what details are you given about how Luce looks? Then extend your analysis – how would you describe Luce emotionally? What philosophy does he seem to adhere to? What values does he represent?

CONSTRUCT . . .
— When you have created a character analysis for Luce, think particularly about his philosophy, or the values he represents. What does Holden appear to want from Luce? What does he ask Luce about? Then think about the subtext to their conversation. What, for example, does Luce recognise that Holden is not conscious of? What do you pick up from their conversation that is implied but not directly stated? Look particularly at the final paragraph of the chapter. How is Holden's behaviour different with Luce here? What particular terms interest Holden in relation to Luce?
— (You may want to connect your discussion of Luce with the Contexts section focusing on psychoanalysis on pp. 176–8. Does Holden's attitude to Luce mirror the text's attitude to

psychoanalysis? Is the text sympathetic to the psychoanalyst or is psychoanalysis satirised, as many topics in the novel are?)

CHAPTER 20
(pp. 135–41)

Focus on: alcohol

REVISE . . .
— Look over your analysis of alcohol in Chapter 10. (If you have not already done so, you may want to attempt the exercise now in order to draw upon the differences between the two chapters). How did you characterise Holden's relationship to alcohol in this section? Look over the different attitudes to drunkenness you identified.

DETAIL . . .
— Now reread Chapter 20, focusing particularly on the treatment of drunkenness here. Think about Holden's behaviour – what does he do in this chapter? How is it characterised in relation to alcohol? To what extent does Holden hold the alcohol responsible for his actions?
— Spend a few moments thinking about the number of different terms you can come up with for drunkenness.
— Use your list to determine how you would characterise Holden's state at this point.

DIFFERENTIATE . . .
— Take your analysis of these two chapters and determine the extent of Holden's deterioration at this point in the novel. How is his condition more severe at this point?
— Think about the difference between 'being drunk' and 'being *a* drunk'. Sketch out your image of 'a drunk' – how well

does it match Holden's behaviour in this later chapter? From your comparison of the two chapters, how would you assess Holden's alteration? In what ways does Holden's increased inebriation suggest a further deterioration in him, emotionally, psychologically, or even socially?

INTERPRET . . .

— Think about how alcohol is used here to suggest Holden's demise. How does it imply his increasing unhappiness? Think about the novel as a whole. Is alcohol, and Holden's drinking, used to suggest the plot's highs and lows, as well as reflecting the deterioration in Holden's mental state?

CHAPTER 21
(pp. 142–9)

Focus on: home

ESTABLISH AND APPLY . . .

— This is the reader's first encounter with Holden's 'home'. Before you embark on your analysis, establish how you understand 'home' and set up a working definition of 'home'. What expectations do you have? What do you associate with 'home'? (Remember to consider the relationship of family to home – is it just a physical space, or does a place stop being 'home' when those you care for are no longer there?)

— When you have established your definition, look over the chapter. To what extent does Holden's 'home' fit your definition?

EVALUATE . . .

— Apply your definition to the text and evaluate the treatment of 'home' at this point in the novel. Why does the text move to Holden's family home and what themes are re-established by this journey? How does this journey affect the novel's plot? Think particularly about the novel's construction – how does this episode fit with the pattern as a whole? For example, it reminds the reader that Holden is still a child who has been expelled from school. Why might Salinger want to highlight this?

CHAPTER 22
(pp. 150–6)

Focus on: Holden

RESEARCH . . .
— Find out what the following psychological terms mean:

• Transference
• Denial
• Repression

INTERROGATE . . .
— When you have established what these terms mean, turn your attention to Holden's conversation with Phoebe here. Can you find examples in Holden's responses to Phoebe? Look, for example, at how he responds to Phoebe's demand that he 'Name one thing' (p. 153) he likes.
— Think about the examples of denial, transference and repression you have found in the novel, and think about their impact on how you read. If, for example, you read a novel presuming the narrator, or speaker, is saying the opposite of what they mean, how does this alter your relationship to the speaker?
— Think particularly about how reading the novel in the light of these terms has changed your attitude to Holden. Do you think he is frequently repressing his desires and fears? Take

one example of repression: what is Holden refusing to recognise when he cites Allie as someone he likes (p. 154)?

EXTEND . . .

— If you are in a group, get into pairs and think about how these terms affect your understanding of Holden as a character. If you read much of what he says as 'denial', or 'repression', how does it change your reading of his character? Do these terms make Holden more comprehensible? If so, how?

CHAPTER 23
(pp. 157–62)

Focus on: family

RECOLLECT . . .

— In this chapter Holden hides when his parents arrive home unexpectedly. Before you begin your analysis, recall an occasion when you have been suspected of doing something you were not allowed to do by your parents, or adult carer. How did you divert their attention? Did you get away with your 'crime'? Was someone else blamed for your misdemeanour? Did they tell on you or did they take your punishment?

— Write a short account of the incident. How would you characterise your feelings at the time? How has your perception of the event altered since its occurrence? Perhaps your sympathies have changed: whereas initially you were concerned only for yourself, perhaps you now recognise others were also affected by the course of events. How has the tone changed – was it a scary incident that is now amusing? Think about narrative style and themes – how would the story differ had it been written by the adult involved?

PARALLEL . . .

— Compare your own story to the incident in the novel. Having used your own account to think about narrative style, tone and the position of the speaker, analyse style, tone and speaker in Chapter 23. Why, for example, is Holden made to overhear his mother's conversation with Phoebe? Who narrates this passage? What themes are highlighted by Holden watching Phoebe get tucked into bed?

— Focus particularly on the end of the chapter, and parallel it with the end of your story. How did you end your story, and in what ways did it frame the story? Did you end on a clear moral, for example?

— Bearing in mind your own narrative, think about this chapter's conclusion: why does Holden break down (pp. 161–2)? How do his tears frame the chapter, and how do they influence your reading of it?

CHAPTER 24
(pp. 163–74)

Focus on: education

CONSIDER . . .

— 'It's this course where each boy in class has to get up in class and make a speech. You know. Spontaneous and all. And if the boy digresses at all, you're supposed to yell "Digression!" at him as fast as you can. It just about drove me crazy. I got an *F* in it (p. 165).' Look at the treatment of education in this chapter, and think about how it is characterised here. Use the following questions to stimulate your analysis:

● Who is Mr Antolini, and what is Holden's attitude to him?
● How does Holden's description of 'digression' epitomise

his difficulty with education? (You may also want to consider 'digression' in terms of Holden's attitude to life and the novel's narrative style.)

● Look at Mr Antolini's description of Holden's education, and his rejection of formal education. How does his version of Holden's future change your reading of Holden (pp. 167–71)?

ASSESS . . .

— Explore Mr Antolini's version of Holden and his possible future. Think in particular about his version of the value of education. Is his assessment of education one that Holden finds valid? If not, why not? Remember to take evidence from the text to back up your conclusion. You could pick words and phrases from anywhere in the novel; just be sure to support your reading.

CHAPTER 25
(pp. 175–91)

Focus on: breakdown

TRACE . . .

— 'There was this magazine that somebody'd left on the bench next to me, so I started reading it, thinking it'd make me stop thinking about Mr Antolini and a million other things for at least a little while. But this damn article I started reading made me feel almost worse' (p. 176). As the novel builds to its denouement, trace the account of Holden's breakdown in this final chapter. How does Salinger suggest Holden's mental collapse? Start with the events of the chapter and think about how the plot and Holden's final journey here suggest his breakdown.

— Then look at the chapter's treatment of his mental state.

How does he describe his feelings? How does he relate to Phoebe? What pattern do these feelings follow as he visits the museum? Where is Holden at the end of the chapter and how does this reflect his state of mind?

DELINEATE . . .

— Having traced Holden's collapse, both physically and through his own descriptions of his state of mind, think about characterising the breakdown itself. Either choose one of the following issues (you may want to assign them to spread the workload and then share your results) or work your way through the topics as they locate different elements of the breakdown in this chapter.

Language

● Does the way the narrative is written change in this chapter – the sentence structure, the narrative voice, whom the narrator is directly addressing? Is the language altered to reflect Holden's collapse – do sentences get shorter, is the language more confused?

Themes

● How is the idea of adolescence presented here? Does it undermine the idea that Holden is having a breakdown, suggesting, rather, that he is a normal adolescent?

● Look at the treatment of family in this chapter, and particularly Holden's relationship with his sister and absent brothers. How does his relationship to them characterise his breakdown? Would Phoebe consider him to be unwell here? In what ways does Salinger imply that Holden's family connections are part of his illness here?

● Focus on the idea of a breakdown. (Again, you may want to relate this task to the Contexts section dealing with psychoanalysis on pp. 176–8.) Tease out the difference

169

between depression and sadness here. Pick examples from
the chapter that demonstrate Holden's depression even
though he appears to be 'happy' or 'carefree' in his behaviour and attitude.

● How is the theme of childhood used to suggest Holden's
collapse? Does he revert to childlike behaviour? (Remember
to cite particular textual examples.)

Focus on: preservation

REMIND . . .

— Look back over your examination of the museum in
Chapter 16. Remind yourself of the importance of the museum
in the text, and its treatment as a repository for memories (both
personal and cultural). If you did not attempt this particular
exercise, you may want to look back over the chapter and
attempt the analysis now in order to benefit your reading of
this penultimate chapter.

EXAMINE . . .

— Taking your analysis of the museum in Chapter 16, examine
its treatment in this chapter. How does the idea of it as a 'childhood' location fit with Holden's meeting with Phoebe there?
Also, consider the idea of 'preservation' in relation to museums.
How do they work to preserve ideas and concepts as well as
objects? Pick a specific example, a museum that you are familiar
with, and consider its role as a preserver.

— When you have thought about the museum and its role in
preservation, return your attention to the novel. What is Holden
attempting to preserve in this encounter with his sister? How
is it paralleled in the function of the museum?

CHAPTER 26
(p. 192)

Focus on: endings

FRAME . . .

— Before discussing the ending itself, compare and contrast this final chapter with the opening chapter of the novel. What thematic concerns are set up at the text's opening and picked up again at its close? Think also about location and narrative voice. Is the novel's opening set in the same place as this final chapter? Who is Holden speaking to in these chapters?

— When you have constructed your responses to these questions, think about how these chapters frame the narrative. Is the majority of the novel concerned with the same themes, and set in the same location?

— Think about the dramatic differences between the first and last chapters and the rest of the novel. Why is the novel framed like this? How does it change your reading of the novel?

CONSIDER . . .

— When you have considered how this chapter, and Chapter 1 form a frame for the text, look particularly at the ending. In what ways does it surprise you as an ending? Who is being addressed? Think about storytelling (if you attempted this exercise in Chapter 1 you may want to remind yourself of your readings). In what ways does this novel refuse to end conventionally?

Looking over the whole novel

QUESTIONS FOR DISCUSSION OR ESSAYS

1. Examine Holden's use of the word 'phony' in the novel. What does Holden perceive to be 'real' as opposed to 'phony'?

2. Using your research into psychoanalysis, discuss the idea

of the novel as a psychoanalytic novel. Is Holden talking to his therapist? If so, how does this change your reading of the text?

3. 'This novel is a handbook on how to be a teenager.' Bearing in mind the historical context of the novel, and the rise of the concept of 'teenage', discuss.

4. To what extent do the elderly characters in this novel represent past values, dismissed both by the protagonist and the reader?

5. 'Holden's behaviour is entirely dictated by his relationship to his family.' Explore the relationship between Holden and his parents, and Holden and his siblings. To what extent are they the motivation for the action and thematic concerns of the novel?

6. Do you consider *The Catcher in the Rye* to be a 'fifties' novel?

7. 'I'm the most terrific liar you ever saw in your life. It's awful. If I'm on my way to buy a magazine, even, and somebody asks me where I'm going, I'm liable to say I'm going to the opera' (p. 14). How does having an unreliable narrator affect your interpretation of this novel?

8. Discuss the different types of intimacy in the novel and Holden's attitude to them.

Contexts, comparisons and complementary readings

Focus on: the fifties

DISCOVER . . .
— *The Catcher in the Rye* is commonly quoted as being representative of 'fifties America'. Using the resources provided, the Internet and with the help of your teacher or group leader, discover what 'fifties America' looked and felt like. You will find the 'American Memory' website at the Library of Congress useful. Which musicians characterise the period? How did people dress in the fifties? What major political events took place in this decade? Which famous novels were written and published in this decade? Who are the fifties icons? The following list suggests some possible starting points for you:

● Elvis Presley
● Zoot suits
● President Truman
● President Eisenhower
● *The Naked and the Dead*
● Marilyn Monroe
● Senator McCarthy

- The Korean War
- Winkle-pickers

— Use the following texts to aid you in your research: *Cracking the Ike Age, Aspects of Fifties America* (1992), edited by Dale Carter; *Secret Agents, the Rosenberg Case, McCarthyism, and Fifties America* (1995), edited by Marjorie Garber and Rebecca Walkowitz.

CHARACTERISE . . .

— Draw on your research to characterise the fifties as a period. What trends, or themes, have you identified? Write a paragraph which highlights the concerns of the fifties, then get together and compare your paragraphs. Have you highlighted different aspects of the decade? If so, think about how this alters the characterisation of the period. For example, if you chose to ignore Korea in your paragraph, how would the inclusion of the Korean War alter the tone of it?

— Be aware in your characterisation of other factors that frame the decade. For example, how would you characterise America's relationship to money in this decade – is it hugely different from the country's attitude to money in the 1940s? Are women represented in a particular way in the fifties? You can use these questions to frame your sketch, or develop your own if you feel particular elements of American culture are neglected here.

DEVELOP . . .

— Apply your characterisation of the fifties to *The Catcher in the Rye*. To what extent does it fit with your representation of the fifties? Would you agree with critics who characterise it as a book representative of this period? If not, in what ways does it complicate your sketch of the fifties?

— *The Catcher in the Rye* was, in fact, written in the 1940s. How does this complicate your reading of it as a fifties text? Does the novel actually predict certain trends? Or does it catch a changing mood, setting up a 'fifties' attitude, without epitomising it?

Focus on: teenagers

LINK . . .
— The discussion of teenagers is directly tied into a concept of the fifties, so if you identified the rise of the teenager in icons such as James Dean, and his role in the film *Rebel Without a Cause* (1955) directed by Nicholas Ray, you were absolutely right. However, the rise of the teenager is a specific cultural event and deserves attention in its own right. When you have completed this section, you might like to combine your research and note how the two concepts interlink.

SKETCH . . .
— Before undertaking your research note down your version of a teenager. What age *is* a teenager? How would you characterise one? What expectations do you have of teenagers? What is their moral code? Do you associate them with rebellion – if so, why, and who are they rebelling against? Is a teenager characterised differently depending on their gender? What statements do you expect from a teenager in relation to popular culture – in terms of hair, music, make-up, demeanour, taste?
— You might like to get together and compare sketches – do your sketches generally agree? Can you form, collectively, a working definition of the teenager?

RESEARCH . . .
— The history of the teenager is both historically and culturally specific. Establish when and where the teenager first

came to be recognised as a type of individual. Would a Victorian English person have understood the term, or a French Edwardian? If you have also worked on Richard Wright's *Native Son*, would you characterise Bigger as a teenager?

— Use the resources in the bibliography as well as the Internet for your research, but you may also want to look at texts such as Peter Everett's *You'll never be 16 again! An Illustrated history of the British teenager* (1986) or for an American take on this phenomenon, Ronald Taylor's *African American Youth: their social and economic status in the United States* (1995) or Franklin Zimring's *American Youth Violence* (1998) You could also watch seminal 'teenage' films such as *Rebel Without a Cause* and from it try to establish how the teenager was initially understood. Also, focus particularly on the relationship between economics and the teenager. How did specific circumstances lead to their 'invention'?

CONTRAST AND EXTEND . . .

— When you have finished your research, contrast your findings with Holden Caulfield. Do you regard him as being an example of the 'teenager'? If so, be specific about the textual evidence that supports your analysis.

— You may then want to combine your examination with your treatment of the fifties. How does your understanding of the history of the teenager inform your attitude to *The Catcher in the Rye*? Does it further define it as a fifties novel?

Focus on: psychoanalysis

ESTABLISH . . .

— Psychoanalysis is a complex discipline with a number of different proponents. Its creator is considered to be Sigmund Freud. Find out who Freud was – you may also want to look at some of his more well-known writings, such as *The Interpretation of Dreams* (1900) or *Beyond the Pleasure Principle* (1920). When you have established a little of his biography, and looked at some of his work, use the following questions to form a working knowledge of psychoanalysis.

● Why is Freud always associated with psychoanalysis – what, for example is a 'Freudian slip'?
● Psychoanalysis involves the patient telling the therapist of his or her dreams. What is the aim of telling these stories?
● Freud worked closely on the relationship between the conscious and the unconscious. What do these terms mean?
● What is transference, and how is it different from denial or repression?
● You may also be aware of practitioners such as Jung and Lacan, but in order to keep your understanding relatively straightforward do not focus on the differences in their practices at this point.

— As well as these questions, use texts such as Julie Rivkin and Michael Ryan's introduction to psychoanalysis in *Literary Theory: An Introduction* (1998). It will set out some of the central tenets of psychoanalysis.

CONSIDER . . .
— When you have begun to research psychoanalysis, and formed a working understanding of some of its principles, turn your attention back to *The Catcher in the Rye*. Do you read it as Holden's session with a psychoanalyst? Is he being cured by talking out his story, and if so, where is the reader placed – are you overhearing a private session? Consider the consequences of this reading for the narrative. Equally, take your analysis of terms such as the 'unconscious', or 'transference'

– does your understanding of such terminology affect your reading? Can you identify Holden's 'unconscious' at work?

TALK THROUGH . . .
— When you have considered the role of psychoanalysis in your reading, talk over your responses. Are you, as a class or group, in agreement about the novel's treatment of psycho-analysis? Is knowledge of the discipline central to your under-standing of this novel? Are we, as readers, keen to know the psychological make-up of characters, what motivates them, what fears are they reacting to? Do we run the risk of for-getting that Holden is a narrative construction? By psycholo-gising Holden, do we confuse him with a real person?

Focus on: the Beats

RESEARCH . . .
— Find out about the group of writers known as 'the Beats'. Leaders among this group were Jack Kerouac (1922–1969) and Allen Ginsberg (1926–1998). In what ways did these writers reject conventional values in life and in literature? How might Holden Caulfield's search for identity and his rejection of what he sees as phony be regarded as a literary example of this process?

Catch-22

IN CLOSE-UP

Reading activities: detailed analysis

Focus on: chapter headings

LOOK AHEAD . . .
— If you look over the titles of the chapters that are coming up, you will see that most of them are names of characters that we encounter in the novel – generally Yossarian's companions in combat. There are exceptions. Occasionally a chapter is headed with the name of a place. Keep an eye out for changes.

I: THE TEXAN
(pp. 7–17)

Focus on: setting and tone

ASK YOURSELF . . .
— The beginning of this novel (or any novel) has to convey to the reader some sense of setting. Readers will also want to be aware of the tone of what they are about to read. What kind of book is this? What do you make of the first sentence? When you have read to the end of the chapter, ask yourself the question about tone again. Is the first sentence to be taken seriously? Where are we? What is it about that

setting that may have some effect on the tone?

— Here are some terms that may help you to focus on the tone of the opening:

- Satire
- Irony
- Understatement
- Comedy
- Criticism
- Bathos

Focus on: repetition and style

LIST AND REMEMBER . . .

— Much of the comic and satiric effect of these opening passages is achieved through the use of repetition and return. Try to keep a list of words, ideas and themes that recur here. As you read through the rest of the book, keep adding to your list. What does this repetition mean to you as a reader? In what ways do you become familiar with what is going on?

Focus on: wordplay

NOTE . . .

— On p. 10 Yossarian says, 'There's no patriotism, that's what it is. And no matriotism, either.' Look up these two nouns. Is 'matriotism' a real word? Why might it not be? How do you know what it means in the context here?

— Keep your eye out for more examples of made-up words or wordplay as you read on through the novel.

Focus on: crazy

CONSIDER THE THEME . . .

— Throughout the novel many characters will call each other 'crazy' or discuss what is 'crazy'. Lunatic and maniac and other 'crazy' words come in too. Keep looking out for them. How would you define crazy? How do the circumstances in which these characters live make a redefinition of 'crazy'?

2: CLEVINGER
(pp. 18–24)

Focus on: understatement and overstatement

RESEARCH . . .

— Research the literary terms 'overstatement' – or 'hyperbole' – and 'understatement' – or 'litotes'. When you have clear definitions in your mind, look over this chapter and make a note of some examples of each. How does this help you to define the tone of the novel as a whole?

Focus on: the normal and the absurd

ASSESS . . .

Look at the passage on p. 19 beginning, 'Clevinger really thought he was right'. Is their situation normal? If so, in what ways? If not, in what ways? How do specific situations change what we consider to be 'normal' behaviour?

Focus on: the cast

MAKE A LIST . . .

— Make a list of every character mentioned in this chapter. Include the people who speak and the people who are spoken about. Include fictional characters – on pp. 22–3. (If you don't know who they are, look them up.) Why do you suppose there are so many names? How do the people only referred to – whether fictional or characters in the book – help to create this world peopled by so many?

3: HAVERMEYER
(pp. 25–35)

Focus on: the absurd

RESEARCH AND COMPARE . . .
— Research the literary term 'the absurd'. There are some suggestions in the Contexts section in this book on pp. 210–11. What does it consist of? Which writers use it? When? Why is it so called? When you have a definition, take another example and compare it with this section of *Catch-22* – the discussion about Orr and the crab apples (pp. 26–7) would be a good place to start. In what ways does this comparison help you to come to an impression of 'the absurd' in literature?

Focus on: food

NOTE . . .
— Havermeyer eats peanut brittle. This is by no means the first time that food has been mentioned. Look back over the book so far and find other examples. Why is food so important in this context? What attitudes to it do the characters have?

AND COMPARE . . .
— Read Oscar Wilde's play *The Importance of Being Earnest* (1895). Check for references to food. How many can you find?

What attitudes do the characters in the play have towards food? Why? How do their attitudes and obsessions compare with those of Havermeyer, Yossarian and the rest?

4: DOC DANEEKA
(pp. 36–44)

Focus on: systems

WHY? . . .
— On pp. 36–7 we are told about the system that Gus and Wes have devised for dealing with anyone who reports sick. What is wrong with their system? How might the account of this particular system relate to the overall theme of systems, rules and regulations in the book as a whole? Where else do you find a 'system' (of a kind) in this chapter?

Focus on: allusions

RELATE . . .
— What do you know about T. S. Eliot and his poetry? Find out what you can. If you know his poem *The Waste Land* (1922), try to work out connections between that work and this novel. In what ways does the allusion to this particular poet enrich the references in Heller's novel? Does it matter that the story told here which happens to include 'T. S. Eliot' is a) a joke, b) a tale about family rivalry and strife, and c) a parable about the absurdity of army systems?

NOTE . . .
On p. 39 there is a quotation from the French '*où sont les neiges d'antan*' – except that is not what the version in *Catch-22* says. Find the source of the reference. How has it been used since?

How is it parodied? Note that 'snow' in the original becomes '*Neigedens*' in reference to Snowden – a companion-in-arms with Yossarian and his company, now dead. Collect references to Snowden. You will find that he becomes very important to the story later on.

5: CHIEF WHITE HALFOAT
(pp. 45–57)

Focus on: digression

THINK ABOUT YOUR OWN REACTION . . .
— Doc Daneeka starts telling Yossarian the story about the married virgin (p. 46). The story involves a number of digressions – Saint Anthony, medical models, low temperatures, etc. The story is delayed – and in fact doesn't get concluded. What effect does this have on you as a reader? Are you intrigued, frustrated, irritated? How does this digressive method relate to the method of the novel as a whole?

Focus on: Catch-22

MAKE A NOTE . . .
On p. 52 the concept of 'Catch-22' is explained. Read this section carefully and bear it in mind as you continue to read, looking for other references to the term.

6: HUNGRY JOE
(pp. 58–67)

Focus on: Catch-22

NOTE THE NEW VERSION . . .
— On pp. 66–7 there is a new description of the terms of
'Catch-22'. Compare this version of 'Catch-22' with the last.
What image are you building up? Setting aside the circum-
stances of the novel, what is your own attitude to these ver-
sions of the 'Catch'?

7: McWATT
(pp. 68–76)

Focus on: irony

RELATE TO THE WHOLE . . .
— 'McWatt was the craziest combat man of them all probably, because he was perfectly sane and still did not mind the
war' (p. 68). Consider the ways in which this statement relates
to the themes of the novel as a whole.

Focus on: characters

REMEMBER . . .
— On p. 71 Nately's whore is introduced. Remember her. She
will be important later on.

8: LIEUTENANT SCHEISSKOPF
(pp. 77–93)

Focus on: adjectives and adverbs

ANALYSE THE LANGUAGE . . .

— Look at the paragraph on p. 77 which begins 'Clevinger knew so much'. There are a number of adjectives listed here describing Clevinger's person and capacities. Carefully note all the adjectives and the adverbs in two or three paragraphs from this chapter. Consider how they are used and what purpose they serve in a) creating characterisation, and b) setting the tone of the novel. You might like also to look out for passages where there are no or very few adjectives and adverbs used, and how that affects the tone of the scene or characters described.

9: MAJOR MAJOR MAJOR MAJOR
(pp. 94–119)

Focus on: wordplay

TAKE THESE THREE EXAMPLES AND EXPAND . . .

— In this chapter we meet Major Major. The first thing we learn is the story of his birth and his naming by his father which involves some play with this idea of ironic repetition. Given that Major Major is being portrayed as the epitome of mediocrity, what is ironic about his name?

— On p. 95 you will find the sentence: 'Some men are born mediocre, some men achieve mediocrity, and some men have mediocrity thrust upon them.' This is a perversion of a famous passage from a Shakespeare play. Find the original. What are the differences? What is ironic about a comparison between

the man the original describes (or purports to describe) and this reinvention?
— Find out about the kinds of roles played by Henry Fonda. Why is it ironic that Major Major should look like this particular film actor?

10: WINTERGREEN
(pp. 120–7)

Focus on: Wintergreen

LOOK BACK . . .
— Go back to find the passage where Wintergreen has already featured. What is his role in the novel? How do the events related here connect to the (brief) picture given at his earlier appearance?

11: CAPTAIN BLACK
(pp. 128–35)

Focus on: the Glorious Loyalty Oath Crusade

INVENT . . .
— Devise a wording for the Glorious Loyalty Oath Crusade. Make it adaptable for any eventuality – whether having your hair cut, or collecting map cases (p. 130). Get your friends to do the same if you are reading this book in a group. Otherwise, invent two or three for yourself. How silly are your oaths? What serious words have you used? What formulae?

RESEARCH AND COMPARE . . .
— Find out about a 'fraternity' movie and watch it if you can.

National Lampoon's Animal House (1978), directed by John Landis, might be a good example. How do the rules and systems and intricacies of initiation in these fraternities compare with the cliques and regulations in *Catch-22*?

12: BOLOGNA
(pp. 136–150)

Focus on: Clevinger

TRANSFORM . . .
— We know that Clevinger is dead (p. 120). Here is a story told about him. Look over this chapter and retell the relevant events, but from Clevinger's point of view. Take no more than a thousand words to do this. Does it make any difference to the tone or character of your story, knowing, by now, that Clevinger has died?

13: MAJOR — DE COVERLEY
(pp. 151–60)

Focus on: characterisation or caricature?

LIST, ANALYSE AND DECIDE . . .
— Look over this chapter, paying particular attention to the descriptions of Major — de Coverley. Note down or under-line all the adjectives, adverbs or phrases that portray his appearance, his manner or his way of behaving. When you have your list, decide if this is a rounded character being shown to the reader here or a caricature?

14: KID SAMPSON
(pp. 161–6)

Focus on: Kid Sampson

ASK YOURSELF . . .
— Why do you suppose that this chapter is called 'Kid Sampson'? How relevant does he seem to the events played out here? Watch out for places where he appears later in the novel.

15: PILTCHARD & WREN
(pp. 167–75)

Focus on: 'importance'

EXAMINE AND EVALUATE . . .
— Captain Piltchard calls a meeting to reprimand Yossarian for instructing Kid Sampson to turn back. He says that no plane is to turn back for an 'unimportant' reason like a defective intercom. We saw these events on p. 167. You might like to look back over that passage.
— In your opinion, is a defective intercom 'important' or 'unimportant'? Why?

ASK YOURSELF AGAIN . . .
— Now read on to the end of the chapter, then ask yourself the same question again.
— How does this one incident relate to the themes of the novel as a whole?

Focus on: fairy-tale imagery

ASSESS . . .

— On p. 172 we are told that Aarfy 'was like an eerie ogre in a dream'. What elements in this chapter contribute to the sense of events taking place as if in a fairy tale, or fantasy, or dream? Is that imagery and vocabulary appropriate here? Why?

16: LUCIANA
(pp. 176–89)

Focus on: Luciana

NOTE AND REMEMBER . . .

— This is the first time that one of the chapter headings has featured a woman's name. Keep a note about Luciana. Close the book and, from memory, write a brief description of her appearance and character in no more than 500 words.

TRANSFORM . . .

— Rewrite the story of Yossarian and Luciana's encounter, but from Luciana's point of view. Then consider how this change of perspective alters the effects created by the story.

Focus on: Catch-22

ANALYSE AND EXPLAIN . . .

— Look at the passage on pp. 183–4 where Yossarian and Luciana discuss marriage. In what ways is Luciana's argument a 'Catch-22' situation? How does this scene relate to the larger themes of the novel as a whole?

17: THE SOLDIER IN WHITE
(pp. 190–202)

Focus on: the soldier in white

LOOK BACK AND COMPARE . . .
— We have met the soldier in white before. Look back at the passage on pp. 10–11 and compare and contrast the two separate narrations of this same episode.

Focus on: Snowden

LOOK BACK, REMEMBER AND NOTE . . .
— We have also heard about Snowden before. Look for those references and make a note of them. Read carefully the short sections on pp. 191 and 198 that are about Snowden. Make a note of them, and remember them. You will need to come back to these passages later.

18: THE SOLDIER WHO SAW EVERY-THING TWICE
(pp. 203–14)

Focus on: comedy

WHY IS IT FUNNY? IS IT FUNNY? . . .
— Look at the scene describing the visit that Giuseppe's family makes to Yossarian – supposing Yossarian to be Giuseppe. Work out why it is funny. Ask yourself if it is funny. Which of the following terms might apply here?

- Comic irony
- Slapstick
- Tragicomedy

- Farce
- Pantomime
- Clowning
- Situation comedy
- Comedy of manners
- Dry humour
- Satire

Focus on: themes

ASK YOURSELF . . .

— 'We're all in this business of illusion together. I'm always willing to lend a helping hand to a fellow conspirator along the road to survival if he's willing to do the same for me' (p. 210). How might the doctor's remark relate to the themes of the novel as a whole?

19: COLONEL CATHCART
(pp. 215–27)

Focus on: repetition and rhetoric

EVALUATE . . .

— Colonel Cathcart is described in fulsome terms. Analyse the vocabulary used and the repetitions and patterns employed in his description. How do these fit with his character? What effect does this style have in influencing your attitude to him?

Focus on: point of view

ASSESS . . .

— The chaplain and Colonel Cathcart speak about Yossarian at the end of this chapter (p. 227). Most of the story so far —

though told in the third person – has focused on Yossarian's perspective. How does this exchange contribute to your assessment of the importance of Yossarian as the central character?

20: CORPORAL WHITCOMB
(pp. 228–39)

Focus on: the chaplain

INTERPRET . . .

— The chaplain becomes increasingly important in the novel from now on. What do you consider his function to be in bringing out the themes and concerns of the novel? How does he help to position the reader's moral viewpoint?

21: GENERAL DREEDLE
(pp. 240–57)

Focus on: obsessions and repetitions

WHAT IS THE POINT? . . .

— Why might Colonel Cathcart be so anxious about Yossarian? Why does he come to the conclusion that Yossarian has too many 'esses' in his name (p. 241)? How rational is his certainty that this indicates that Yossarian is 'subversive', 'seditious', etc.? Does it make sense in terms of the world of the novel? Does it make sense in terms of your own view of the world?

CONSIDER . . .

— Once you have thought about Cathcart and his obsessions, look at the passage on p. 248 where Moodus and Dreedle speak about Dreedle's 'delectable' nurse. How are they also drawn into (irrelevant) obsessions? What do any of these passages suggest about the character of the novel's world?

22: MILO THE MAYOR
(pp. 258–74)

Focus on: Snowden

LOOK BACK AND FORWARD . . .
— Snowden is mentioned at the beginning of this chapter. Look back over the novel and your notes on the Snowden episode and references to it so far. Continue making the notes and collecting these allusions.

23: NATELY'S OLD MAN
(pp. 275–87)

Focus on: fathers

MAKE LINKS . . .
— This chapter is titled 'Nately's old man'. He is the man in the brothel, but there are also a number of references here to Nately's father – that is, his 'old man'. Nately and the old man have long discussions about the respective characters of various nations, and about the nature of patriotism. What does 'patriot' mean? What is the connection to the idea of fathers and nationhood? Make as many links as you can between these themes in relation to this episode.

24: MILO
(pp. 288–306)

Focus on: April

RESEARCH AND COMPARE . . .

— April is mentioned several times in the opening paragraph. Look up 'April' in a dictionary of quotations. How many allusions can you identify in this paragraph? Look out for literary references in this chapter and in subsequent chapters. What functions do they serve?

25: THE CHAPLAIN
(pp. 307–28)

Focus on: the chaplain

CONSIDER AND ASSESS . . .

— What is the function of the chaplain's role in the novel? How do you know? How much do you trust his point of view, and why?

26: AARTY
(pp. 329–36)

Focus on: the role of women in wartime

COUNT . . .

— Several women are mentioned in this chapter, including, near the beginning, Nately's whore. We never know her name. Is that significant? Nurse Duckett also figures here. How do the men treat her? What is the men's attitude to the women they encounter? Count up how many chapters are headed with titles that include a woman's name. Count up how many women characters there are in the novel overall.

TRANSFORM . . .
— Write ten sentences about women and war.
— Then write ten sentences about women and war, but write them as opinions that might be expressed by ten different women that you know (that is, anyone – your mother, a political figure, your teacher, yourself).
— What does this exercise suggest about conventional ideas about gender stereotypes and war, as against real people's real opinions and attitudes?

RESEARCH AND COMPARE . . .
— Read the first and last chapters of Susan Hill's novel *Strange Meeting* (1971) where there is a portrait of Hilliard's mother. The novel is set during the First World War. Or else read the first section of Jeanette Winterson's *The Passion* (1987). It is set during the Napoleonic wars at the beginning of the nineteenth century. How does the portrayal of women in wartime in either or both of these novels compare with the pictures given in *Catch-22*?

27: NURSE DUCKETT
(pp. 337–50)

Focus on: Nurse Duckett

REWRITE . . .
— Read the chapter through, then close the book and write a description of Nurse Duckett in no more than 500 words. How far do you feel that you have an image of her character? To what extent might she be stereotyped and in what ways?

Focus on: dreams

INTERPRET . . .

— There is a long discussion about dreaming and the nature and character of dreams in this chapter. How do dreams and dreaming reflect on the themes and concerns of the novel as a whole?

28: DOBBS
(pp. 351–64)

Focus on: 'crazy'

CONSIDER OVERALL . . .

— A number of characters accuse each other of being 'crazy', as they do throughout the novel. As with the exercise in Chapter 1, think again about what 'crazy' means. How many different contexts can you list where the word might be appropriate? Where is it often used, but may not be appropriate? How does 'crazy' relate to the themes of the novel as a whole?

29: PECKEM
(pp. 365–78)

Focus on: jargon, platitudes and meaning

CONNECT . . .

— On p. 366 we are told that General Peckem likes to use particular kinds of words and phrases. Think about the words and phrases that are given as examples here. In what way is Peckem's language inadequate to the situations it is meant to describe? Why are clichés, jargon and platitudes so unsatisfactory in communicating in a meaningful way? Look up each of the terms to give yourself a substantial working definition. Why might it be that such platitudes are more likely to be used in time of war? What other class of persons might routinely use such terms? Choose from this list:

- Politicians
- DJs
- Poets
- Children

RESEARCH . . .
— Look through a couple of pages of any newspaper or magazine. How many examples of clichés, jargon or platitudes can you find? Do they serve any purpose? How do your chosen examples help you to develop a perspective on the language employed by certain characters in *Catch-22*?

Focus on: Orr

LOOK BACK AND FORWARD . . .
— Orr has disappeared. Look back to see where else he has figured and what function he serves in the structure of the novel as a whole. Look out for further references to him and his fate as you read.

Focus on: allusion

COMPARE . . .
— There is a reference on p. 371 to Shakespeare's *Hamlet*. If you have read the play consider how apt this comparison may be.

30: DUNBAR
(pp. 379–90)

Focus on: irony

ASK YOURSELF . . .
— Consider these two statements:

'"Boy," he said coldly, "you sure must be in a pretty bad state. You ought to go home"' (p. 382).
'Nurse Duckett found Yossarian wonderful and was already trying to change him' (p. 387).

— What is right – or wrong – about these two statements? Find others like them. Try to work out the method and technique which makes comic irony the chief mode of the narrative tone of the novel. How does this technique work? Look for other examples in the novel and analyse their method and effectiveness.

31: MRS. DANEEKA
(pp. 391–6)

Focus on: Mrs Daneeka and the other women

LOOK OVER, CONTRAST AND COMPARE . . .
— Compare the portrayal of Mrs Daneeka with that of Luciana and/or Nurse Duckett.

Focus on: officialdom and condolence

RESEARCH AND COMPARE . . .
— Read the letter sent to Mrs Daneeka on p. 396. What do you make of it? If you have read Sebastian Faulks's First World

War novel *Birdsong* (1993) look again at Part 4, section 12, where an official letter of condolence is sent by a commanding officer to the family of a soldier who has been killed. Compare the two letters. In what ways are they similar? Do you imagine that the bereaved – in either case – might be consoled by such letters?

32: YO-YO'S ROOMIES
(pp. 397–402)

Focus on: Kid Sampson

DISCUSS . . .
— What role does Kid Sampson play in focusing the concerns of the novel overall?

33: NATELY'S WHORE
(pp. 403–12)

Focus on: Nately's whore

CONTRAST AND COMPARE . . .
— 'Nately's whore' is the fourth major woman character to be introduced into the action of the novel. How does she compare with the previous three?

WHAT DO YOU THINK? . . .
— 'She wondered vaguely why they wanted her to laugh when they laughed, and why they wanted her to enjoy it when they made love to her. It was all very mysterious to her, and very uninteresting' (p. 405). What do you think the answer is? Why is she uninterested? Why might they care?

34: THANKSGIVING
(pp. 413–21)

Focus on: Thanksgiving

FIND OUT AND DECIDE . . .
— If you do not already know, find out about the American tradition of Thanksgiving. In what ways is this particular occasion of that celebration a perversion of the values that it should represent?

35: MILO THE MILITANT
(pp. 422–31)

Focus on: the system

INVESTIGATE THE RHETORICAL IRONY . . .
— On pp. 426–8 Milo explains his system of trade to Colonel Cathcart. How would you describe his story? What kinds of words and images are used? Are they:

- Romantic
- Exotic
- Enticing
- Fairy tale
- Practical
- Banal
- Appropriate?

— How does Cathcart's reaction – to the fact that the absence of Milo will make the whole system collapse – relate to the conclusions and argument of the novel as a whole?

36: THE CELLAR
(pp. 432–46)

Focus on: Catch-22

CONNECT . . .
— On pp. 437 the chaplain is accused of not writing in his own handwriting. How does the concept of 'Catch-22' connect to this scene?

37: GENERAL SCHEISSKOPF
(pp. 447–9)

Focus on: the absurd

LOOK BACK . . .
— Return to your research on 'the absurd' from Chapter 3. What in this scene is 'absurd'?

38: KID SISTER
(pp. 450–63)

Focus on: kid sister

JUDGE . . .
— Think over the times when you have seen or heard about Nately's whore's kid sister so far. What function does she serve in the novel?

39: THE ETERNAL CITY
(pp. 464–82)

Focus on: the pilgrimage

MAKE CONNECTIONS . . .
— This chapter is called 'The eternal city' – a term for Rome, the centre of the Catholic world, the home of the Vatican and the Pope, and the destination for many devout pilgrims. Yossarian makes a journey around the city. In what ways are the scenes that he encounters a summary of all that has gone before in the novel? Is he on a quest? If so, what is he looking for – both practically and metaphorically?

40: CATCH-22
(pp. 483–92)

Focus on: Catch-22

RELATE . . .
— Why do you suppose this chapter is given the same title as that of the book? Make a case for the microcosm of this chapter relating to the novel as a whole.

41: SNOWDEN
(pp. 493–504)

Focus on: Snowden

WHY? . . .
— Why do you suppose we return to the story of Snowden's death – in its full horror – just at this point in the novel? Look

back over the novel – from p. 39 on – to all the references to Snowden. (You should have made a note of them as they occurred.) Now piece together all of those references. How far does this experience of Snowden's death colour and explain all of Yossarian's actions and attitudes?

Focus on: adjectives and adverbs

ANALYSE THE LANGUAGE . . .

— Look at the paragraph on pp. 503–4 that begins 'But Snowden kept shaking his head and pointed at last'. There are some adjectives and adverbs used here. Carefully note them. Consider how they are used and what purpose they serve. You might have undertaken the exercise for Chapter 8 which asked you to look at adjectives and adverbs. You could look back at the notes you made then (and for subsequent passages) to see how the use, abuse or non-use of adjectives and adverbs affects the tone of any one passage.

42: YOSSARIAN
(pp. 505–19)

Focus on: Yossarian

IMAGINE AND ASSESS . . .

— What do you think happens to Yossarian? Has he made the right decision? Why? Read the last sentence of the novel and make a case for its appropriateness in view of the events, and terms of the novel as a whole.

Looking over the whole novel

QUESTIONS FOR DISCUSSION OR ESSAYS

1. Consider *Catch-22* as a novel of 'the absurd'.

2. '*Catch-22* gives the impression of having been shouted on to paper.' Do you agree?

3. Consider the note at the beginning of the text of *Catch-22*: 'The island of Pianosa lies in the Mediterranean Sea eight miles south of Elba. It is very small and obviously could not accommodate all of the actions described. Like the setting of this novel, the characters, too, are fictitious.' Relate this note to the themes and concerns of the novel.

4. '*Catch-22* is a pilgrimage.' Discuss.

5. What is the importance of EITHER the character of Snowden OR the character of the chaplain to the novel as a whole?

6. 'Yossarian lives.' Why?

7. 'We're all in this business of illusion together. I'm always willing to lend a helping hand to a fellow conspirator along the road to survival if he's willing to do the same for me' (p. 210). Consider EITHER 'this business of illusion' OR 'the road to survival' in relation to the themes of *Catch-22* as a whole.

8. Analyse the workings of the humour in *Catch-22*.

9. Assess the portrayal of war and wartime life in *Catch-22*.

10. How many 'catches' are there in the novel? How does the 'catch' appear and in what different guises in the novel as a whole?

11. What part do women play in *Catch-22*?

12. The narrative is told in a disordered, tangential way. What does this technique imply about the nature of time in *Catch-22*?

Contexts, comparisons and complementary readings

Focus on: numbers

LIST . . .

— '"That's some catch, that Catch-22," he observed. "It's the best there is," Doc Daneeka agreed' (p. 52). On pp. 51–2 the term 'Catch-22' is explained for the first time. Other versions of it pepper the novel and you should have been looking out for these and keeping a list of them. The term is one that has entered popular vocabulary since the publication of Heller's novel, and is generally recognisable in the English-speaking world, as well as being a term understood in other languages. How often do you hear someone refer to 'a Catch-22' situation, meaning an impossible position, or a dilemma in which one cannot win?

— Make a list of other phrases from titles or other sources that use a number and which have similarly become a familiar term as a slogan or a shorthand for some understood reference. Examples might include: 1066 and all that, 9/11, Page 3, 69, 42, first class, 1003, 40 days and 40 nights, 11 November, 2000, the 49th parallel, *The Thousand and One Nights*, *The Third Man*. How many others can you find? Consider how these titles or numbers function in the collective cultural memory. How quickly do you recognise the reference? How easily do others understand the allusion?

Focus on: catchphrases

LIST . . .
— 'Catch-22' in itself has become a 'catchphrase'. What other titles can you think of that have similarly entered the language? Examples might include: *Utopia, Oranges Are Not the Only Fruit, Much Ado About Nothing*. Again, with any of your examples, consider how quickly you recognise the reference. How easily do others understand the allusion?

WHY DO THEY WORK? . . .
— Remember that Joseph Heller worked for some years writing advertising copy. Look again over the whole novel and pick out phrases or sentences that resemble the kinds of slogans or pithy summaries that you find in advertising. What are the key requirements that make a good slogan? Make a list. You might include such elements as: brevity, memorability, precision, alliteration, assonance.
— Once you have made your list, consider the literary uses of such phrases, or methods of using language. What effects might they have on the reader – or listener, or viewer?

Focus on: the absurd

RESEARCH . . .
— Find out about the technical literary term 'the absurd' and the kinds of drama or literature that it relates to. In what period was it mainly employed? Why might it have occurred as a

phenomenon at that time? What techniques does it include? What philosophies might it imply? Use the definition in the glossary, but look up other sources as well.

DETERMINE . . .
— How might any or all of the constituents of 'the absurd' that you have identified connect to the methods, subject and form of Heller's *Catch-22*?

RESEARCH AND COMPARE . . .
— Look for books and plays that use the form of the Absurd. Some titles that could be useful for comparison are: Lewis Carroll's *Alice's Adventures in Wonderland* (1865); Oscar Wilde's *The Importance of Being Earnest* (1895); Samuel Beckett's *Waiting for Godot* (1952); Edward Albee's *Zoo Story* (1959); Harold Pinter's *The Caretaker* (1960); or Joe Orton's *What the Butler Saw* (1969).
— Read any of these works and compare and contrast with Heller's *Catch-22*. In what ways might they use similar methods? Make a list. These headings may be useful:

- Arbitrariness
- Unwarranted authority
- Uniforms
- Systems
- Lack of individual independent thought
- Repetition
- Rules
- Inconsequence
- Surprising juxtapositions
- Lack of control

Focus on: moral choice

RESEARCH AND COMPARE . . .

The contingencies of war often give rise to situations of difficult moral choice, but sometimes cruelty and lack of compassion mean that 'choices' forced on individuals are not only extreme and testing, but also arbitrary and – in some senses – impossible and even absurd.

— Read William Styron's novel *Sophie's Choice* (1976). When you arrive at the revelation of what 'choice' was offered Sophie and how she 'chose', compare her circumstances with those of Yossarian and the other soldiers stationed on Pianosa. How 'free' are they? What 'choice' do they actually have? How much 'choice' do many people have in deciding how they live – whether in a war scenario or not?

Focus on: the Second World War in modern memory

RESEARCH AND CONSIDER . . .

— In the second half of the twentieth century – and still in the twenty-first century – the subject of the Second World War and different soldiers' experience of it dominates in both Hollywood films and in many European-made films. Pick one or two such films – whether one made soon after the events they purport to depict (whether 'true' or fictional) or one made years later. You might even find it helpful to take one from each period – so, say, *The Great Escape* (1962) directed by John Sturges, and *Saving Private Ryan* (1998) directed by Steven Spielberg – and compare the differences.

— How does the presentation of the circumstances of war in the films you have chosen compare with the presentation of a similar situation in *Catch-22*? These headings may help you to focus your analysis:

- Irony
- Propaganda
- Heroism
- Criticism
- Pathos
- Bathos
- Anger
- Sentimentality

Focus on: war and comedy

ASK YOURSELF . . .

— Quite often, a characteristic of film and television treatments of war situations is the employment of comedy. Look for places where the experience of war is presented in a comic way.

— Examples of such treatment might include *M.A.S.H.*, the American film and television series about a medical unit in the Korean War, or *Dad's Army*, the British television comedy series. What in the situation presented in such cases makes it possible to deal with the subject of war in an amusing way? Why might anyone wish to deal with war as if it were funny? How does comedy inform and underlie your experience of reading *Catch-22*?

Focus on: film and stage adaptations

COMPARE . . .

Heller dramatized *Catch-22*, and the novel has also been adapted for the screen. Find out about Heller's adaptation. Then you might start by visiting the Heller archive at the University of South Carolina's website. Compare the adaptation with the novel. Alternatively, watch the 1970 film adaptation directed by Mike Nichols. (The screenplay was by Buck Henry.) How successfully does this adaptation capture the mood of the novel?

VINTAGE
LIVING
TEXTS

Reference

Glossary of literary terms

Absurd A term applied to works in drama and prose which view the human condition as essentially absurd. Literature of the Absurd has its roots in Expressionism and Surrealism. Since the 1940s, absurdist literature has become closely associated with the existentialist view of the universe as possessing no inherent value or meaning, and of the human condition as anguished as well as absurd.

Ambivalence When your attitude to a person or event is unresolved or unsure because you feel both positive and negative about something. For example, both loving and hating someone leaves you ambivalent towards them.

Antithesis Two ideas that are the direct opposite of one another. It is when two concepts embody values which contrast in every way. For example, the antithesis of peace is war.

Bathos The effect created, intentionally or not, when a passage that attempts to be elevated in tone instead drops into the trivial or the ridiculous, or when an elevated style is combined with everyday subjects. It can also describe the effect created when an author employs trite sentimentality to manipulate a reader's sympathies.

Binary opposition Related to the idea of two concepts being opposed to one another, but the important factor with binary oppositions is that you have to understand both of the contrasting values to understand the opposition. For example, in order to understand the colour 'red' on a traffic light you have to understand 'green'. If all lights were red there would be no opposition and the light means nothing. Or, if no one explains to you that red = stop and green = go, then the lights would make no sense.

Characterise To describe your understanding of a person, event or context. You pick particular terms that convey to a new reader what you consider to be the most important factors when observing your example. For instance, you might characterise Santa Claus as 'jolly and fat', or 'bearded and generous'.

Chronology An arrangement of dates and times in the order in which they occurred, which gives you a sense of a sequence of events. It is particularly useful when novels are fragmented and the order of events is difficult to remember.

Circumscribe Literally means to draw a line around something, but here it suggests the events or idea which surround or control a person or event. So you could say that a vicar is circumscribed by religious values.

Cliché An idea, image or expression that has been so overused that it has lost much of its original impact and become stale.

Comedy of Manners Comedy that figures stock characters in complicated social situations, and which relies largely on witty dialogue.

Commodity Commonly understood as an 'article of trade'. In this context it is employed to suggest that an individual has been turned into an article of trade. For example, women are treated as a commodity when a pimp makes an arrangement with a customer for a prostitute. She is the object of their trade.

Conceptualise To take your ideas and examples and explain them as a concept. You could talk about a rose as an object, and about the associations it has, such as Valentine's Day. You would conceptualise it by talking about it as representing the concept of 'Love'.

Contextualise To take a set of events or individual characters and link them. By linking the disparate ideas or events you create a 'context' for the action or character.

Denouement A shorthand for the final solution in a play or novel. It is the crisis point at which the plot's twists and turns are explained to the audience. For example, the denouement of *Othello* is Desdemona's murder and the explanation of Iago's trickery.

Disenfranchise To deny a community access to representation. To enfranchise is to give a community representation in court. Therefore, the importance of this term is that it suggests that separation.

Emasculation/emasculate Literally means to castrate or weaken, but here the sense is that masculinity is being undermined. It is to feminise a man, for example by suggesting that he is unmasculine because his female partner supports him, or is more able to do his work than he is.

Empathy The sensation of participating in the physical existence of a person or object outside of oneself. It is often used interchangeably with 'sympathy' to mean 'fellow feeling', sharing in the emotional state of another, but it can refer to purely physical movements. One may feel sympathy for a person in distress, but only empathy for the tumult of a roaring sea.

Empirical Describes an argument or opinion based on facts or observations as opposed to theories and ideas.

Empower To give an individual authority, licence or power ideologically or thematically. For example, women are empowered by the right to vote as it gives them a 'voice' in the community as their views are represented.

Epitomise To encapsulate or sum up, in a word or phrase, a complex idea.

Extended metaphor A metaphor that runs throughout a paragraph or chapter, or even an entire poem, play or novel. For example, the metaphor of animalistic sex runs through all of Iago's vocabulary in *Othello*. He repeatedly refers to the idea of Desdemona and Othello as coupling animals.

Farce A type of comedy that uses exaggerated characters in ludicrous situations, usually involving physical humour, e.g. Charlie Chaplin comedies.

Genealogy A family descent, or history. It is another term for a family tree, but is not necessarily mapped out as family trees are.

Genre A French term referring to the different forms or kinds of literature, and implying the existence of certain fixed characteristics in each kind.

Historicise To locate an idea in a historical context. For example, using the historical events of slavery to understand the history the novel refers to.

Holocaust Literally means 'burnt offering', but it is employed in the context of the Second World War as meaning 'a massive sacrifice, or wholesale destruction'. It is employed here to mean the wholesale destruction of people.

Hyperbole An extravagant overstatement, usually used to create a comic effect.

Impunity To be exempt from punishment or injury, to be able to continue a particular course without any external control or rules dictating to you.

Inscription A name in a book. This suggests ownership or gives something meaning, just as a name is used to suggest belonging.

Irony/to ironise To express an idea by using the opposite terms. So, when 'fish and chips' is described as top-class French nouvelle cuisine the speaker is probably being ironic. It is also used to convey information to a particular audience. In order to be rude about someone's food, you might compare it to the worst meal you have ever eaten. However, if the cook has never heard of the restaurant the sentence 'This food is almost as good as the pizza I ate in Giovanni's!' could be taken as a compliment. The irony is reserved for those who know Giovanni's.

Jargon The terminology of a particular group or discipline, which may exclude those who are not familiar with the idiom.

Juxtapose To place two contrasting ideas, phrases or styles next to one another. A chapter may juxtapose characters or settings, for example.

Litotes A form of understatement, frequently with a negative assertion, and usually with ironic intentions, e.g. 'a not unpleasant experience' meaning, 'it was delightful'.

Metaphor A figure of speech that ascribes the qualities (literally or imaginatively) of one thing to another. Unlike a simile, which asserts a comparison, a metaphor asserts that one thing is the other, e.g. 'morning is a new sheet of paper for you to write on' – Eve Meriam.

Naturalism Sometimes used to mean the selection of materials and of literary manner that gives the illusion of actual experience, like realism. Naturalism also embodies the philosophical notion that human beings have no souls, but are entirely the product of a combination of genetic inheritance, which brings compulsive instincts, and of social and economic environment.

Nostalgia A sentimental desire for what is past and irrecoverable.

Object In literary theoretical discourse, the role attributed to women in identity-formation, in binary opposition to 'subject', the role attributed to men. This stems from Simone de Beauvoir's observation that in much Western discourse 'man' is at the centre, and 'woman' is only defined in relation to him. This is why she perceives that, traditionally, women are 'the second sex'.

Overstatement See hyperbole.

Pathos The effect of evoking feelings of pity or sympathetic sorrow in a reader or audience.

Personification/personify This has two meanings. 1) To give an object or animal human characteristics, such as describing the sun's smile. 2) To sum up in a phrase or description an attitude or set of ideas.

Platitude A banal and trite remark, especially if it is offered as if it were significant.

Polemic A narrative style and, literally, a contentious argument. In a literary context it also suggests an argument that is designed to be contentious.

Privilege To highlight or foreground, placing a particular idea or set of ideas at the forefront of the reader's attention.

Rape fantasy A critical term referring to a dominant cultural theme in Western culture where people assume and fear – wrongly – that a certain kind of man wishes to rape a certain kind of woman. Note that this is not to do with individual experience, nor to do with personal desire. It is a cultural myth which may or may not be adopted by certain persons and societies for their own political ends. In Margaret Mitchell's novel *Gone with the Wind*, for instance, there is a prevalent 'rape fantasy', shared by the white slave owners, that all black men want to rape white women. This notion is an instrument of control both for the women – they are made to feel afraid and dependent on the protection of their white menfolk – and for the black slaves – they are construed as brutal and animalistic and therefore in need of strict policing.

Satire A literary technique that illuminates and ridicules human weaknesses such as folly, vice or greed. Satire often combines many other methods of humour such as sarcasm, wit, irony and caricature, and employs laughter as a weapon. Much satire is considered political because it seeks not only to amuse its audience but also to make them realise truths about society.

Scopophilic An individual is scopophilic when his attention is focused primarily through the eyes. Someone who reacts to the world first and foremost through sight.

Semantics Semantics focus on the relationship of language to meanings.

Simile A figure of speech that explicitly compares one thing with another, using 'like' or 'as', to clarify the image, e.g. 'O my love's like a red, red rose' – Burns.

Situation Comedy A form of comedy that presents stock situations and easily recognisable character types, and often involves elements of farce. A common type of television comedy, e.g. 'Fawlty Towers' and 'Absolutely Fabulous'.

Slapstick Knockabout comedy, including boisterous and clownish physical buffoonery.

Stream of consciousness A narrative that is written to mirror the internal processes of thought, the ideas that run through our minds even when we are apparently silent. It becomes a continual narrative.

Subject In literary theory, a notion closely bound up with identity-formation. A person as 'subject' suggests free agency, but this notion is complicated by the fact that the person is also subject to social conditioning. Much feminist theory is based on the observation that Western cultural discourse often makes man the 'subject' and woman the 'object'. The consequences are that women are often placed in secondary, contingent or marginal positions.

223

Transparent Clear or obvious.

Trilogy A trilogy is a set of three. It initially meant three Greek tragedies that were performed in quick succession. It is now taken to mean three texts which are all complete in their own right but are connected thematically.

Trinity A group of three, or a union of three persons. However, it is usually understood as a Holy Trinity, the three parts of which are: God the Son (Jesus), God the Father (God) and God the Holy Spirit.

Understatement See litotes.

Voluble Fluent, suggesting that someone speaks well, and often at length, on a particular topic, or in a particular language.

Biographical outlines

Richard Wright

1908 Born in rural Mississippi. Later moved to Memphis and then to Chicago.

1932–44 Joined the Communist Party and worked for the Federal Writers Project and wrote for political journals and papers.

1937 Moved to New York.
'Blueprint for Negro Writing', a Marxist based essay, published.

1938 *Uncle Tom's Children* published, based on his Mississippi childhood.

1940 *Native Son* published. The film version starred Wright as Bigger Thomas.

1941 *Three Million Black Voices* published.

1945 *Black Boy*, an autobiography, published.

1947 Moved to Paris, after breaking with Communism in 1944.

1953 *The Outsider* published.

1960 Died in Paris.

1977 *American Hunger*, a sequel to *Black Boy* published.

1978 *The Richard Wright Reader* published.

Harper Lee

1926 Born Nelle Harper Lee in Monroeville Alabama. She was a childhood friend of the writer Truman Capote.

1961 *To Kill a Mockingbird* published. Awarded the Pulitzer Prize.

1962 *To Kill a Mockingbird* made into a film starring Gregory Peck.

J. D. Salinger

1919 Born Jerome David Salinger. Raised in New York.

1934 Entered at the Valley Forge Military Academy. Later served as an infantryman in the Second World War and was awarded five battle stars.

1948 Published stories in *The New Yorker* including 'A Perfect Day for Bananafish'.

1951 *Catcher in the Rye* published.

1953 *Nine Stories* published. Retitled in the UK as *For Esme – with Love and Squalor and Other Stories*.

1961 *Franny and Zooey* published.

1963 *Seymour: An Introduction* and *Raise High the Roofbeam, Carpenters* published.

1997 *Hapworth 16, 1924* published.

Joseph Heller

1923 Born in Brooklyn, New York City.

1939–45 Served in the American Air force flying 60 combat missions during the Second World War.

1961 *Catch-22* published.

1967 *We Bombed in New Haven*, a play, produced.

1970 *Catch-22* filmed.

1974 *Something Happened* published.

1979 *Good as Gold* published.

1984 *God Knows* published.

1986 *No Laughing Matter* (with Speed Vogel) published.

1988 *Picture This* published.

1994 *Closing Time* published, a sequel to *Catch-22*.

1999 Died in New York.

Select bibliography

WORKS BY RICHARD WRIGHT
Uncle Tom's Children (1938: Harper Perennial, New York, 1993)
Native Son (1940: Vintage, 2000)
Black Boy (1945: Vintage, 2000)
Savage Holiday (1954: University of Mississippi Press, Jackson, Mississippi, 1994)

CRITICISM
Ann Algeo, *The Courtroom as Forum: Homicide Trials by Dreiser, Wright, Capote and Mailer* (New York, Peter Lang, 1996)
Richard Abcarian, *Richard Wright's A Native Son: A Critical Handbook* (Wadsworth Publishing Company, California, 1970)
James Baldwin, *Notes of a Native Son* (Corgi Books, London, 1969)
Donald B. Gibson ed., *Five Black Writers: Essays on Wright, Ellison, Baldwin, Hughes, and LeRoi Jones* (New York University Press, New York, 1970)
Fritz Gysin, *The Grotesque in American Negro Fiction* (Franke Verlag, Bern, 1975)
Kenneth Kinnammon and Michael Fabre eds., *Conversations with Richard Wright* (Jackson University Press, Mississippi, 1993)
Kenneth Kinnammon ed., *New Essays on Native Son* (Cambridge University Press, Cambridge, 1990)

Edward Margolies, *The Art of Richard Wright* (Southern Illinois University Press, Illinois, 1969)

R. W. Yoshinobu, *Critical Essays on Richard Wright* (G.K. Hall, Massachusetts, 1982)

USEFUL WEBSITES

www.olemiss.edu/depts/english/ms-writers

WORKS BY HARPER LEE

To Kill a Mockingbird (1960: Vintage, 2000)

To Kill a Mockingbird (The Folio Society, London, 1996)

USEFUL WEBSITES

http://mockingbird.chebucto.org/bio.html

http://www.educeth.ch/english/readinglist/leeh/

CRITICISM

Jean Armstrong, *To Kill a Mockingbird*, (Macmillan Master Guides, London, 1987)

Graham Handley, *To Kill a Mockingbird* (Penguin Passnotes, Penguin, 1985)

Claudia Durst Johnson, *Understanding To Kill a Mockingbird: a student casebook to issues, sources and historical documents* (The Greenwood Press, Literature in Context series, Westport Connecticut and London, 1994)

Claudia Durst Johnson, *To Kill A Mockingbird: Threatening Boundaries* (New York: Twain, 1994)

Jill P. May, 'Censors as Critics: TKM as a Case Study', *Cross-Culturalism in Children's Literature: Selected papers* (CLA, Pace University, 1988)

Colin Nicholson, 'Hollywood and Race: To Kill a Mockingbird', *Cinema and Fiction: New Modes of Adapting* (Edinburgh University Press, 1992)

Terry Morgan, *To Kill a Mockingbird* (Tynron Press, Instant Revision series, Thornhill, 1991)

Cathy Kelly Power, *Thirteen Ways of Looking at a Mockingbird: A*

Collection of Critical Essays (Georgia State University, 1996)

WORKS BY J.D. SALINGER
The Catcher in the Rye (1951: Penguin, London, 1994)
Nine Stories (1953: Warner Books, New York, 1991) published in London as *For Esme With Love and Squalor* (Penguin, London, 1994)
Franny and Zooey (1961: Penguin, London, 1994)
Raise High the Roof Beam, Carpenters, and *Seymour, an Introduction* (1963: Penguin, London, 1994)

USEFUL WEBSITES
http://www.levity.com/corduroy/salinger.htm
http://dir.salon.com/books/feature/2000/10/02/salinger/index
.html
www.salinger.org

CRITICISM
Paul Alexander, *Salinger, A Bibliography* (Renaissance Books, Los Angeles, 1999)
Ian Hamilton, *In Search of J. D. Salinger* (Heinemann, London, 1988)
Pamela Hunt-Steinle, *In Cold Fear, The Catcher in the Rye, Censorship Controversies and Post War American Character* (Ohio State University Press, Ohio, 2000)
Marvin Laser & Norman Fruman, *Studies in J. D. Salinger, Reviews, Essays, and Critiques of The Catcher in the Rye and other fiction* (Odyssey Press, New York, 1963)
Sanford Pinsker, *The Catcher in the Rye, Innocence Under Pressure* (Twayne's Masterwork Series, New York and Oxford, 1993)
Sanford and Ann Pinsker, *Understanding The Catcher in the Rye: a student casebook to issues, sources and historical documents* (The Greenwood Press, Connecticut, 1999)
Jack Salzman ed., *New Essays on The Catcher in the Rye* (Cambridge University Press, Cambridge, 1991)

WORKS BY JOSEPH HELLER
Catch-22 (1961: Vintage, London, 1994)

Something Happened (1974: Vintage, London, 1995)

Good as Gold (1979: Simon and Schuster, New York)

Joseph Heller & Speed Vogel, *No Laughing Matter* (Jonathan Cape, London, 1986)

Picture This (Macmillan, London, 1988)

Closing Time (Simon and Schuster, New York, 1994)

Now and Then: From Coney Island to Here (Simon and Schuster, London, 1998)

Portrait of an Artist as an Old Man (Scribner, London, 2000)

USEFUL WEBSITES

The Joseph Heller Archive at the University of South Carolina, www.sc.edu/library/spcoll/amlit/heller.html

Dmoz.org/Arts/Literature/Authors/H/Heller

www. gradesaver.com/Classic Notes/Authors/about_joseph-heller.html

CRITICISM

Nicholas Bayley, *York Notes on Joseph Heller's Catch-22* (Longmans, London, 1987)

Harold Bloom ed., *Joseph Heller's Catch-22* (Chelsea House, Modern Critical Interpretations Series, Northam, 2001)

David M. Craig, *Tilting at Morality: Narrative Strategies in Joseph Heller's Fiction* (Wayne State University Press, Michigan, 1997)

Rudolf Fritsch, *Absurd oder grotesk? Uber literarische Darstellung von Entfremdung bei Beckett und Heller* (Lang, Frankfurt am Main, 1990)

Joseph Heller, *Catch-22*, with an introduction by Malcolm Bradbury (David Campbell, London, 1961)

Brenda M. Keegan, *Joseph Heller: A Reference Guide* (Prior, London, 1978)

Robert Merrill, *Joseph Heller* (Twayne Publishers, New York, 1987)

James Nagel ed., *Critical Essays on Joseph Heller* (G.K. Hall, Boston, Massachusetts, 1984)

Sanford Pinsker, *Understanding Joseph Heller* (University of South Carolina Press, South Carolina, 1991)

Stephen Potts, *From Here to Absurdity: The Moral Battlefields of Joseph Heller* (Bongo Press, San Bernardino, California, 1982)

Robert M. Scotto, *Three Contemporary Novelists: An Annotated Bibliography of Works by and about John Hawkes, Joseph Heller and Thomas Pynchon* (Garland, New York, 1977)

David Seed, *The Fiction of Joseph Heller: Against the Grain* (Macmillan, Basingstoke, 1989)

Adam J. Sorkin, *Conversations with Joseph Heller* (University of Mississippi, 1993)

Harold Swardson, *Fighting for Words: Life in the Post modern University* (Verlag Die Blaue Enle, Essen, 1999)

GENERAL CRITICISM

William Andrews et al. eds, *The Oxford Companion to African American Literature* (Oxford University Press, 1977)

Bernard Bell, *The Afro-American Novel and its Tradition* (University of Massachusetts Press, Massachusetts, 1987)

Deborah Cameron, *Feminism and Linguistic Theory* (Macmillan, London, 1992)

Hazel Carby, *Race Men* (Harvard University Press, 1988)

Dale Carter ed., *Cracking the Ike Age, Aspects of Fifties America* (Aarhus University Press, Aarhus, 1992)

Carol Fairbanks, *Black American Fiction: A Bibliography* (Scarecrow Press, London, 1978)

W. J. Cash, *The Mind of the South* (New York, Alfred A. Knopf, 1941)

George M. Fredrickson, *The Black Image in the White Mind. The debate on Afro–American Character and Destiny 1817–1914* (Harper & Row, New York, 1971)

Marjorie Garber & Rebecca Walkowitz, *Secret Agents, the Rosenberg Case, McCarthyism, and Fifties America* (Routledge, London, 1995)

John Guillory, *Cultural Capital, The Problem of Literary Canon Formation* (University of Chicago Press, Chicago, 1993)

Sandra Gunning, *Race, Rape and Lynching, The Red Record of American*

Literature 1890–1912 (Oxford University Press, Oxford, 1996)

Lynn Higgins ed., *Rape and Representation* (Columbia University Press, New York, 1991)

A. Robert Lee, *Black American Fiction since Richard Wright* (Hill and Wang, New York, 2000)

Henry Louis Gates Jr., *Figures in Black, Words, Signs, and the 'Racial' Self* (Oxford University Press, Oxford, 1987)

Neil R. McMillen, *Dark Journey: Black Mississippians in the Age of Jim Crow* (University of Illinois Press, 1990)

Toni Morrison, *Birth of a Nation 'hood: Gaze, Script and Spectacle in the O. J. Simpson Case* (Vintage, London, 1997)

Toni Morrison, *Race-ing Justice, En-gendering Power: Essays on Anita Hill, Clarence Thomas and the Construction of Social Reality* (Pantheon, New York, 1992)

Adam Newton, *Facing Black and Jew, Literature as Public Space In Twentieth Century America* (Cambridge University Press, Cambridge, 1999)

Sanford Pinsker, *Between two Worlds: The American Novel in the 1960's* (Whitston Publishing Co., New York, 1980)

Sanford Pinsker, *Conversations with Contemporary American Writers* (Rodopi, Amsterdam, 1985)

Julie Rivkin and Michael Ryan, *Literary Theory: An Introduction* (Blackwell, Oxford, 1998)

Roger Rosenblatt, *Black Fiction* (Harvard University Press, Massachusetts, 1976)

Peter Stallybrass, *'Patriarchal Territories: The Body Enclosed,' Rewriting the Renaissance*, Ed. Margaret W. Ferguson, Maureen Quilligan, and Nancy J. Vickers (Chicago and London: University of Chicago Press, 1986)

Laura Tunner, *Intimate Violence: Reading Rape and Torture in Twentieth Century Fiction* (Indiana University Press, Indiana, 1994)

The editors

Jonathan Noakes has taught English in secondary schools in Britain and Australia for fifteen years. For six years he ran A-level English studies at Eton College where he is a house-master.

Margaret Reynolds is Reader in English at Queen Mary, University of London, and the presenter of BBC Radio 4's *Adventures in Poetry*. Her publications include *The Sappho Companion*, *The Sappho History* and (with Angela Leighton) *Victorian Women Poets*.

Louisa Joyner completed her Ph.D. at the University of London. She is an editor and critic.

ALSO AVAILABLE IN VINTAGE LIVING TEXTS

❑	*American Fiction*	0099445069	£6.99
❑	*Martin Amis*	0099437651	£6.99
❑	*Margaret Atwood*	009943704X	£6.99
❑	*Louis de Bernières*	0099437570	£6.99
❑	*Sebastian Faulks*	0099437562	£6.99
❑	*John Fowles*	0099460882	£6.99
❑	*Susan Hill*	0099452189	£6.99
❑	*Ian McEwan*	0099437554	£6.99
❑	*Toni Morrison*	009943766X	£6.99
❑	*Salman Rushdie*	0099437643	£6.99
❑	*Jeanette Winterson*	0099437678	£6.99

- All Vintage books are available through mail order or from your local bookshop.
- Payment may be made using Access, Visa, Mastercard, Diners Club, Switch and Amex, or cheque, eurocheque and postal order (sterling only).

❑❑❑❑❑❑❑❑❑❑❑❑❑❑❑❑

Expiry Date:＿＿＿＿＿＿ Signature:＿＿＿＿＿＿＿＿＿＿＿＿

Please allow £2.50 for post and packing for the first book and £1.00 per book thereafter.

ALL ORDERS TO:
Vintage Books, Books by Post, TBS Limited, The Book Service,
Colchester Road, Frating Green, Colchester, Essex, CO7 7DW, UK.
Telephone: (01206) 256 000
Fax: (01206) 255 914

NAME: ＿＿＿＿＿＿＿＿＿＿＿＿＿＿＿＿＿＿＿＿＿＿＿＿＿＿＿

ADDRESS:＿＿＿＿＿＿＿＿＿＿＿＿＿＿＿＿＿＿＿＿＿＿＿＿＿

＿＿＿＿＿＿＿＿＿＿＿＿＿＿＿＿＿＿＿＿＿＿＿＿＿＿＿＿＿＿

＿＿＿＿＿＿＿＿＿＿＿＿＿＿＿＿＿＿＿＿＿＿＿＿＿＿＿＿＿＿

Please allow 28 days for delivery. Please tick box if you do not wish to
receive any additional information.
Prices and availability subject to change without notice. ❑